CU00729721

COAST & CASTLES

THE COMPLETE GUIDE

2003/2004

By Mark Porter

Accommodation, food and drink,
history, route and maps

Newcastle - Edinburgh

Coast & Castles Complete Guide
1st Edition: 2003

Copyright: Baytree Press

Published by Baytree Press,
Bridge St,
Rothbury,
Northumberland NE65 7SG
T:+44 (0) 7767 893790

E: mark@coast-and-castles.co.uk
W: www.coast-and-castles.co.uk

ISBN 0-9544827-0-0
Distributed by: Cordee Books and Maps
3a de Montfort Street
Leicester LE1 7HD
T:+44 (0)116 254 3579
W: www.cordee.co.uk

CONTENTS

INTRODUCTION

Welcome to the first edition of Coast & Castles: The Complete Guide, a comprehensive account of where to stay, where to eat and where to drink as you make your way between Newcastle and Edinburgh, through some of Britain's most breathtaking countryside. With colourful descriptions, maps and illustrations of the route, it also offers historical sketches of the places you will visit (N.B. the technical data such as distances and mapping is at the end of the book).

This guide is primarily - but not exclusively - aimed at the cyclist; much of the terrain it covers, including some stretches on minor roads, is ideal for walkers.

Starting near Hadrian's Wall, the journey ends in the Scottish capital, thus linking the Tyne estuary with the Forth.

The route is called Coast & Castles because the hundred or so miles of shoreline it follows, threaded through Northumbrian fishing villages and vast sandy beaches, is dotted with forts and castles such as Warkworth, Bamburgh and Lindisfarne. When it veers inland up the Tweed valley and into the homeland of Sir Walter Scott, you will encounter some of Scotland's finest heritage, before finally cycling into Edinburgh from the commanding heights of the Moorfoot Hills.

Your hosts have been chosen for their understanding of the cyclist's needs, their warm welcome, high standards of accommodation and the fact that your bikes should be safe.

Like sirens to willing seafarers, the many pubs and restaurants beckon the weary traveller. We have singled out the best ones, so if you're taking your time (and believe me, it's worth it) you should take full advantage. You can also check them out on our website.

This book also caters for those who wish to do the journey in a couple of days. After peddling 100 miles in a day, you'll be looking for a good meal and somewhere comfortable to rest your tortured limbs.

The Coast & Castle (C&C) – referred to on the blue waysigns as Route 1 – is based largely upon the route compiled by a charity called Sustrans, a dedicated team of eco-friendly cycle warriors who are in the process of turning many of Britain's minor byways and pathways into a national network of cycle routes.

Where we have occasionally thought it appropriate, we suggest different directions, but would advise anyone tackling the C&C to buy the Sustrans map, available from many tourist information centres or from the charity's headquarters at 35 King Street, Bristol BS1 4DZ **T:**+44 (0)117 929 0888, and on their website: www.sustrans.org.uk Our map profiles are courtesy of Sustrans, as are the town maps of the tricky bits.

While the route is pretty well signposted, it is as well to have a map. There will be occasions when you miss the blue and white panels. New Ordnance Survey Landrangers have the route marked, and if you have the space to store six of them, the maps you need are: 88, 81, 75, 74, 73 & 66.

Also, please try to book accommodation, meals and packed lunches in advance. If you want to avoid disappointment, try not to arrive unannounced expecting beds and meals to be available. And if you have to cancel a booking, please give as much notice as possible. Otherwise, be prepared to forfeit your deposit (this is at the discretion of the proprietor). Suggestions for additional addresses are most welcome, together with your comments.

Please note that the information given in the Complete Guide was correct at the time of printing and was as supplied by the proprietors. No responsibility can be accepted by this independent company as to the completeness or accuracy of all entries, nor for any loss arising as a result. It is advisable to check the relevant details when booking.

Whilst we have a small gay section for Newcastle and Edinburgh (see pages 17 & 120-1), our guide is limited in between. However most accommodation owners now live in the 21st century, and for further information, please see www.rainbowholidays.com or www.pinklinks.co.uk/accommodation

FOREWORD

Warkworth, Bamburgh, Lindisfarne, Berwick-upon-Tweed, Norham and Edinburgh are as tantalizing a roll call of castles as you will ever find. Mix this with the riverside escape from the great city of Newcastle to the wide sea views over Whitley Bay and Druridge Bay, and the empty roads across the border you get on close to cyclists' paradise as you can in these isles. The start is especially good if Gateshead's Millennium Bridge "blinks" and I am very fond of the uncertainty of the tidal crossing to Holy Island where the temptation to be marooned in the refuge tower struggles with the desire to move on. Take time at Berwick to see the ramparts that defended this frontier town – a town which was until recently still "officially" at war with Russia!

The fact that Sustrans could devise a route from England to Scotland which crosses the Tweed on the Union Bridge from Scotland back to England is quite a feat and I am particularly pleased that St Boswells, Melrose and Galashiels, three romantic places off the beaten track to the north, are all central to the Coast & Castles Route. Edinburgh is one of those cities which is striking from a great distance, as well as memorable, and you will find that the view from the Moorfoot Hills is all that you might have wished for.

I hope that you enjoy this route, a cycling journey made all the more possible with Mark Porter's excellent guide, and that you will return home refreshed and inspired to cycle more, and to persuade your friends and neighbours to do so too.

John Grimshaw,
Director & Chief Engineer
SUSTRANS

ACKNOWLEDGEMENTS

Many thanks to the Newcastle Gateshead Initiative for allowing us to use their picture library. The same goes to Berwick Borough Council, and Lorna Suthren in particular, for allowing us free use of her archive, and for being so generally helpful. Similarly Edinburgh & Lothian Tourist Board for their assistance, not to mention all the kind help afforded by the Scottish Borders Tourist Board in Selkirk. The name of that well known photographer Graeme Peacock cropped up on the credits in Northumberland. His website (www.graeme-peacock.com) is a treasure trove of great local images. Thanks also to Tom Burnham, of Trade Partners UK, without whom this book would not have happened; and Dave Coyle, whose expertise and patience were invaluable. And a big thanks to Sustrans, whose field officers were unfailingly obliging. See p.129 for the Sustrans card stamping scheme and commemorative C&C T-shirt.

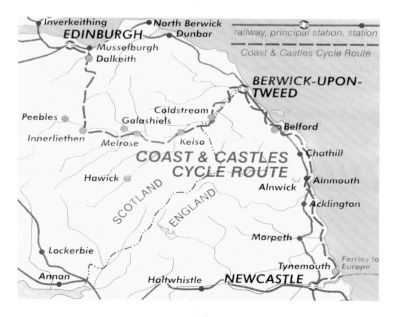

Where to start

My view, and that of Sustrans, is that south to north makes most sense – i.e. Newcastle to Edinburgh. The wind is generally more favourable, and Tyneside, with its bustling port, ferry terminus, airport and mainline railway station, make it a natural starting point. But that does not discount doing it the other way round; this book should be comprehensible taken back to front, just like the Sustrans map. However, going north to south would also entail going through places like Blyth, Byker and Wallsend at the end of the ride, rather than having the majestic final sweep into Edinburgh, past Arthur's Seat and the Old Town. No disrespect to these places, but most would feel that their gritty industrial charm does not put them top of the list of attractions the Coast & Castles route has to offer.

On finishing the route...

If you do not feel like cycling back to Newcastle after the 200-mile journey, then jump on a train. They are fast, regular and bike-friendly (there's no extra charge for the bike). To book train seats, see details below.

Getting here

Rail

There are direct train services from most cities in Britain to Newcastle Central Station. It is served by Great North Eastern Railways (GNER), Virgin Cross Country and Regional Railways. It takes 2 hours 45 minutes from London, and 1 hour 20 minutes from Edinburgh.

To book train seats between Edinburgh and Newcastle, call either Virgin **T:**+44 (0)8457 222333 or GNER **T:**+44 (0)8457 225225, or phone the national rail enquiry service on **T:**+44 (0)8457 484950 with any other queries.

Road

Newcastle is easily accessible. The A1(M) goes through the middle of it. If you are coming by car, there is limited parking at Newcastle station, and the charge is £5 a day. There's also the 635-space Tyne Square Car Park nearby, which does special rates for five or seven day parking of around £3 a day.
T:+44 (0)191 243 8294

The **Tourist Information** Centre in Newcastle is
T:+44 (0)191 277 8000, and in Edinburgh it is
T:+44 (0)131 332 2433
W: www.visitscotland.com

Air

Newcastle Airport is only 20 minutes from the city centre and there are regular and frequent links to many European cities, including Amsterdam, Brussels and Paris, along with international connections to the rest of the world. There are also direct flights to Aberdeen, Birmingham, Gatwick, Heathrow, Wick, Dublin and Belfast.
T:+44 (0)191 286 0966
E: www.newcastleairport.com

Sea

The International Ferry Terminal at Royal Quays is the North of England's main sea link with Scandinavia and Continental Europe and operates regular passenger services from Norway, Sweden and the Netherlands.
Fjord Line **T:**+44 (0)191 296 1313
DFDS Seaways **T:**+44 (0)900 333 000/111

Part I

NEWCASTLE – UPON – TYNE

Ever since the Romans arrived 2,000 years ago Newcastle has been a hub of trading activity. The town grew up around Pons Aelius, a Roman fortification about 10 miles inland from the North Sea. For the last 800 years a booming trade in wool, leather and coal have brought the city prosperity.

Now it's one of the most 'happening' places in northern Europe. A magnet for shoppers and clubbers, diners and drinkers, it boasts some of Britain's finest architecture. Recent restoration projects have included Norman fortifications, 16th century merchant houses and the great neo-classical designs of Grainger Town. There are also art galleries, museums and concert venues aplenty.

Newcastle and Gateshead, its neighbour on the south bank of the Tyne, have been voted England's best short break destination. The two towns have also teamed up to contend for the European Capital of Culture in 2008, a link symbol-ised by the arcing strand of the new Gateshead Millennium Bridge across the Tyne.

In short, it is the perfect place to start this cycling Odyssey, and we would recommend stopping here overnight and sampling its urban delights before setting off up the banks of the Tyne in search of the Northumberland coast.

PLACES OF INTEREST

Castle Keep, Castle Garth, St Nicholas St **T:** +44 (0)191 232 7938 Built by Henry II between 1168-78 on the site of the so-called New Castle, built in 1080 by William the Conqueror's son, Robert Curthose. It was after this edifice that the town was named. The New Castle itself was constructed on the site of the Roman Pons Aelius (Bridge of Hadrian). Admission: £1.50, 50p concessions.

Baltic Centre for Contemporary Art, Gateshead Quays **T:** +44 (0)191 478 1810 Opened in July 2002, BALTIC is the major new centre for contemporary visual art and stands grandly above the water on the south bank. Five galleries and more than 3,000 square metres.

Music Centre Gateshead, Gateshead Quays **T:** +44 (0)191 443 4666 Sir Norman Foster's contribution to the Geordie quayside, a music complex catering for classical, folk, jazz, brass and choral.

Gateshead Millennium Bridge. Takes walkers and cyclists from Newcastle's Quayside across to Gateshead Quays and BALTIC Square. The bridge opens and closes like a giant eyelid, allowing shipping to pass. Spectacularly lit at night, like many who inhabit these once louche purlieus.

Grainger Town – a rejuvenated architectural treasure containing Many of the city's top shops.

Chinatown – around Stowell St. Restaurant standard is good and prices reasonable.

There are plenty of hotels and guest houses. The Jesmond area, just north of the centre, is full of places to stay and lively night spots. If you're overnighting in the city, there are hotels near the waterfront, down on the fashionable Quayside.

For a full list of hotels, call the **Tourist Information Centre** on **T:**+44 (0)191 277 8000 or get hold of the Newcastle Gateshead Accommodation Guide ngi@ngi.org.uk by calling the Newcastle Gateshead Initiative on **T:**+44 (0)191 243 8800.

When in Tyneside, many like to stay around the Quayside. It is close to **Central Station** where the ride officially starts (or ends), so I have concentrated my entries in this area. The atmosphere is vibrant and the pubs and restaurants are among the best in town; however the hotels, as in most city centres, can be expensive.

PUBS

Crown Posada, The Side. **T:**+44 (0)191 2321269
Known locally as The Coffin because it is long and narrow, this is probably the city's best pub. There's no TV, and any music comes either from an old gramophone or the mouths of revellers. There are stained-glass windows, interesting ceilings, wood-clad walls and six excellent ales. Legend has it that the pub was bought by a Spanish sea-captain for his mistress.
(See ad on p.123)

Bridge Hotel, Castle Square. **T:**+44 (0)191 232 6400
Big pub looking across at the castle keep. Nestles into the side of the mighty high level bridge. Patio garden at the rear encircled by the old town wall affords great views of the river.

The Old George Inn, Cloth Market. **T:**+44 (0)191 269 3061
One of the 'Toon's' oldest establishments, you reach it down a cobbled back alley. Despite being in the middle of the frantic Bigg Market, where every night is like New Year's Eve in other towns, it is a grown-up drinking spot.

Duke of Wellington, High Bridge **T:**+44 (0)191 261 8852
This pub is a one-room wonder, stocking lots of fast changing ales from all over the country. Used to be run by a 50-stone landlord, one of the biggest men in the world, whose bulk would have barred him from entering the Posada.

RESTAURANTS

Indian

Leela's, 20 Dean St. **T:**+44 (0)191 230 1261
Delicate southern Indian cuisine. Cooking is of a very high standard. This small family concern manages to exude sophistication and intimacy at the same time.

Vujon, 29 Queen St. **T:**+44 (0)191 221 0601
Another classy curry joint. It is next door to Asha Raval (0191 232 7799) which also comes highly rated in Asian circles.

Chinese

Lau's Buffet King, 44-50 Stowell St. **T:**+44 (0)191 261 8868
If you want to pack in the protein for the following day's ride, this is the place. It's a hugely popular 'all-you-can-eat' that seats 300.

King Neptune, 34-36 Stowell St. **T:**+44 (0)191 261 6657
Award winning food. Sumptuous surroundings. You can't go too far wrong anywhere in Stowell St.

Italian

La Riveria, Gateshead Quays. **T:**+44 (0)191 477 7070
Recent addition to the Gateshead side of the Tyne. Great location and wide choice of Italianate cooking.

Marco Polo, 33 Dean St. **T:**+44 (0)191 232 5533
Friendly, efficient service. Traditional fare, dim lighting. Marco's is an institution.

Uno's, 18 Sandhill, Quayside. **T:**+44 (0)191 261 5264
Offers some cheap and cheerful choices. Popular with celebrities.

Modern

Café 21, 19-21 Queen St, Quayside. **T:**+44 (0)191 222 0755
Simply one of the best restaurants in the north east, you need to book well in advance.

Quay 35, 35 The Side, Quayside. **T:**+44 (0)191 232 3848
Early evening 2-course special for £11 or £12. Cosy spot, Quay 35 has a good selection of fish, meat and vegetarian options.

World Food

Kublai Khan, The Side, Quayside. **T:**+44 (0)191 221 1596
Only place in the area to do Mongolian food. Served buffet style, you select your ingredients and a Mongol Chinese emperor will cook it for you.

Heartbreak Soup, Quayside. **T:**+44 (0)191 222 1701
Latin American/Mexican/ Central American fare. Eclectic and vibey.

GAY & LESBIAN

There's a 'gay village' in the west of the city just five minutes' walk from Central Station.

Betty's, 2 Marlborough Crescent. **T:**+44 (0)191 261 7772
Intimate little café/bar. Good hot and cold meals.

The Dog, 5 Marlborough Crescent. **T:**+44 (0)191 221 0775
Classy little pub favoured by gays and straights alike.

Heavens Above, 2 Scotswood Rd. **T:**+44 (0)191 261 0488
Cool and trendy night spot straddling the top of The Yard.

Mims Bar, 3-5 Waterloo St. **T:**+44 (0)191 232 2014
Cosy downstairs bar popular with the older crowd. Men only feel about the place.

Miss Carras, The Cluny, 36 Lime St. **T:**+44 (0)191 230 4474
Laid back ladies spot. Live bands and high jinks.

Rockies, 78 Scotswood Rd. **T:**+44 (0)191 232 6536
Very popular gay bar with a permanent party feel about it.

The Yard, 2 Scotwood Rd. **T:**+44 (0)191 232 2037
Smart establishment for younger and older men alike, split over two floors. The older guys tend to inhabit the downstairs, while Heaven's Above (see previous page entry) attracts the trendoids.

HOTELS

Premier Lodge, The Exchange, Quayside. **T:**+44 (0)870 700 1504
All 136 rooms £49.95.

Travel Lodge, 4 Forster St, Quayside. **T:**+44 (0)191 261 5432
All 120 rooms £59.95. Family room will sleep three if the double bed
is shared!

Youth Hostel, 107 Jesmond Rd. **T:**+44 (0)191 281 2570
£11.40 for under-18. £14.65 for over-18. Members only, but non-
members can join up on arrival. *(see ad on p .126)*

The George Hotel, 88 Osborne Rd, Jesmond.
T:+44 (0)191 281 4442/2943
Small family run concern with 16 rooms. From £35.

Kenilworth Hotel, 44 Osborne Rd, Jesmond.
T:+44 (0)191 281 8111
Family business run by keen cyclist. 12 bedroom from £38.

Da Vinci's, 73 Osborne Rd, Jesmond. **T:**+44 (0)191 281 5284
Good, cheap wildly Italian restaurant with 15 bedrooms from £40.

Westland Hotel, 27 Osborne Avenue, Jesmond.
T:+44 (0)191 281 0412 Small, friendly, family run hotel. Secure area for
cycles. 14 bedrooms from £25 a night.

NEWCASTLE TO THE COAST

Left out of Central Station **(map p.134)** and follow signs down Forth St to the north bank of the Tyne. Turn left. The stretch from the Millennium Bridge is known as the 'Golden Mile of Culture' on both banks, because of the number of galleries, museums and concert venues.

Head due east along the Tyne, past the law courts, smart hotels, wine bars and riverside apartments, where new Geordie money flaunts itself. Beyond there, as the river loops past Byker and round towards Wallsend, towards the shipyards and the giant cranes, the old Tyneside re-emerges. It's goodbye to the metropolis, with its acres of glass and stainless steel, and hello to fine relics of a recently bygone age. There are 60s high rise flats and men in cloth caps walking whippets and tending pigeon lofts. The route (marked C2C and 72) leads continuously along the north bank, past the Segedunum Roman Fort, to the end of the Hadrian's Wall National Trail.

WALLSEND is ideal for the Hadrian's Wall experience. The fort at Segedunum was recently brought back to life at a cost of £9 million, and displays the only Roman bath-house in Britain. About four miles from the ferries, it is another possible start point.

HADRIAN LODGE HOTEL,
Hadrian Road,
Wallsend,
Tyne & Wear
NE28 6HH.
Manageress: Claire Stubbs.
T:+44 (0)191 262 7733
F: 0191 263 0714
W: www.hadrianlodgehotel.co.uk
Rooms: 24 - 9 singles, 9dbl, 6 twin, 1 family
B&B: £38.50 single; £49.50 double or twin.
Family from £50
Evening meal: from £6.55 to £14.95
Packed lunches: £5
Distance from C&C: 30 metres.

The Lodge is a modern and serviceable spot. It can secure up to 6 bikes and all the rooms are en-suite. Although a small businessman's sort of establishment, it is smart and well run.

A couple of miles down river on the opposite bank sits **Jarrow**, home of the Venerable Bede, and the Bede's World Museum. It was also the starting point for the Jarrow March. Two hundred hunger strikers descended upon London in 1936 and made one of the most striking political statements in British working class history.

As you approach the Royal Quays North Sea Ferry Terminus make sure you follow the signs (easily missed) and go to the LEFT of the Wet 'n' Wild water centre (you can't miss it – the giant flume tubes look like part of some space-age factory). Follow the path through landscaped public gardens in which an incongruous cluster of wooden sea groynes stand, as if awaiting tidal erosion. Turn left just beyond them, by a faded waysign – do not head back in the direction of the Amsterdam and Bergen ferry terminal – and go through the modern housing estate. To the right pleasure craft and fishing boats should be bobbing around at their moorings.

Keep following the C2C, Route 72 and Route 10 signs (they are clustered together) and you will find yourself passing through another modern housing estate. You are now in **North Shields**, erstwhile home of comedian Stan Laurel.

Following the signs, descend a steep flight of stone steps to the fish quays. You will arrive outside a pub called the Chain Locker, opposite the ferry terminus to South Shields. The view across the Tyne on a good day is worth a pause. You can see, in the far distance, the elegant 19th century façade of the clock tower of South Shields town hall.

Cafes, stores and splendid fish & chip restaurants run the length of the North Shields Quays. This is where Danish and Polish sailors used to integrate thoroughly with the local community at a den of iniquity called the Infamous Jungle, now known as the Collingwood Buildings.

An excellent watering hole is the **Shiremoor House Farm** *Middle Engine Lane, New York, North Shields. Good beer and food* **(see ad on p.124)**

TYNEMOUTH

You soon round the point where the North Sea meets the Tyne. Welcome to Tynemouth. You pass the 11th century Priory and Castle, and the handsome statue of the man who really won the Battle of Trafalgar in 1805, Admiral Lord Collingwood. Nelson's unassuming and undersung deputy single-handedly took on five French warships for a full hour before the rest of the English fleet caught up. He assumed command upon Nelson's death half-way through the battle, and is Tynemouth's most famous son.

This is a stylish little haven centred upon Front St, a handsome wide avenue built for eating, drinking and promenading. The village is a conservation area of architectural gems from the 18th and 19th centuries.

The stretch of shore from here, through **Cullercoats** and up to **Whitley Bay (map p.135)**, is known as Newcastle's Côte d'Azur. You will note that there is cycle parking in Tynemouth and Whitley Bay, just over a mile up the coast.

Aerial view of Tynemouth Priory

PLACES TO EAT

Sidneys, Percy Park Rd, **T:**+44 (0)191 257 8500.
Giorgio's Pizzeria & Restaurant, Front St. **T:**+44 (0)191 257 3758
Marshall's Fryery at the Priory, Front St. **T:**+44 (0)191 257 2435
The Gate of India, 40 Front St. **T:**+44 (0)191 258 3453
Gibraltar Rock Carvery East St. **T:**+44 (0)191 258 5655.

PUBS

Fitzpatricks, Front Street, is a handsome establishment. It is one of eight pubs in the small town. Has a changing selection of hand-pulled ales. Food served. **(see ad on p. 124)**

The Turks Head, Front St., otherwise known as the Stuffed Dog because of Willie the Scottish collie, whose 130 year old taxidermised remains sit in a glass box looking at the bar. Willie came down from the Scottish Borders with a herd of sheep and a shepherd, but somehow got separated from them and spent the rest of his life waiting and pining in Tynemouth for his lost master. A tale of epic proportions told in detail on a plaque. Good Courage Directors, regular guest ales. Food served all day.

ACCOMMODATION

GRAND HOTEL,
Nigel and Angela Hastie,
Grand Parade,
Tynemouth,
NE30 4ER.
T:+44 (0)191 293 6666
F:+44 (0)191 293 6665
E: info@grandhotel-uk.com
W: www.grandhotel-uk.com
Rooms: 44
B&B: From £32.50 - £90
Evening meal: £19
Packed lunch: £10
Smoking: Yes
Distance from C&C: On route. Hotel has bar.
Three star hotel originally built in 1872 as a home for the
Duchess of Northumberland, the Grand Hotel is situated on
a cliff top with stunning views of the coast.

No.61 GUEST HOUSE & TEA ROOMS
Carol & Ron Scott,
61 Front Street,
Tynemouth,
NE30 4BT.
T:+44 (0)191 257 3687
Rooms: 5 en-suite
B&B: from £40 for single to £55 for double with balcony
and sea view.
Packed lunch: £5
Smoking: No
Distance from C&C: On route.
Surrounded by pubs and restaurants. Fine Georgian building
recently and sensitively restored. There's a warm welcome for
cyclists and a secure garage for their bikes. The rear rooms
look over the mouth of the Tyne.

WHITLEY BAY

It is impossible not to notice that this resort, with its Pleasure Dome, Spanish City and seaside villas, is geared up for tourism and little else. Every other building offers food, drink or accommodation. Or all three. Whitley Bay is a striking seaside resort, and in the past was a thriving holiday resort for tourists. It is currently attempting to rediscover its former glory, when smart Geordies would jockey for position on Newcastle Coast's promenade.

PUBS

Fitzgeralds
Half-timbered Victorian pub. Good food and drink and a lively night spot. *(see ad on p.122)*

Briar Dene
'A former tollhouse with a well-earned reputation for good quality beer and food,' according to the Good Beer Guide (CAMRA Books: £12.99). It overlooks St Mary's lighthouse and the sea. Serves good food. *(see ad on p.122)*

Rockcliffe Arms
Attractive one-roomed pub with stained-glass, and two distinct drinking areas separated by a partition. Proper 'locals' pub.

EATING

There are dozens of good Indian restaurants, so it seems invidious to single any particular ones out. Indeed there are dozens of eateries covering a whole gamut of international cuisine.

ACCOMMODATION

WINDSOR HOTEL
Trevor and Tina Hastie,
South Parade,
Whitley Bay,
NE26 2RF
T:+44 (0)191 251 8888 **E:** info@windsorhotel-uk.com
F:+44 (0)191 297 0272 **W:** www.windsorhotel-uk.com
Rooms: 70 - 2 single, 34 dbl, 26 twin and 8 family.
B&B: From £30 to £65
E. meal: From £9.75 to £25
Packed lunch: From £5
Smoking: Yes
Drying facilities. Pubs and restaurants just feet away.
Close to sea and town with award winning restaurant. All rooms are en-suite and there is car and bike parking plus storage. There's also a Metro link to Newcastle and the airport, and it's just 5 miles from the ferry terminals.

REX HOTEL
Manager: Gillian Innes
Promenade,
Whitley Bay,
NE26 2RL
T:+44 (0)191 252 3201 **E:** reception@rex-hotel.com
F:+44 (0)191 251 4663 **W:** www.rex-hotel.com
Rooms: 69 - 13 dbl, 19 single, 10 family, 6 triple, 4 quad, 19 twin
B&B: from £39, less if sharing; group bookings taken
Evening meal: £5 - £12.50.
Packed lunch: £5
Smoking: Designated areas.
In the of heart Whitley Bay, surrounded by pubs and restaurants, this is one of the oldest establishments in town. Many of the rooms face the sea, and there's a lively night life. Ideal for groups.

Blyth windmills

From here it is a fairly straightforward four mile trundle up to **Seaton Sluice** along the pavement-cycleway, though you will notice an absence of signposting. Follow the path along **Whitley Sands** before taking the cycle path running alongside the A193 dual carriageway. After half a mile the road turns sharp left, but you go right, taking the track down to the nature reserve. You will see **St Mary's Lighthouse** and its causeway.

Make your way up through the dunes and the radio masts (keeping the masts to your left) and shortly you are in Seaton Sluice.

*A good spot for lunch and a pint is the **Delaval Arms** at **Old Hartley**, just before Seaton Sluice. The route almost takes you into the front door of this nice old fashioned hostelry. Good range of local real ales **T:**+44 (0)191 237 0489*
Food served 12-3 and 6-8.

WATERFORD ARMS,
SueGriffin,
Colleywood Bay Rd.
Seaton Sluice,
Whitley Bay,
NE26 4QZ
T:+44 (0)191 237 0450
Rooms: 6 – All en-suite. 3 doubles, 1 twin, 1 single, 1 family.
Evening meal: £3.95 to £16
Packed lunch: £3 to £5
Smoking: In designated areas.
"Home from home," says Sue. "Good home cooked food and baking. Our afternoon teas are great. This is a friendly place with good real ale." The Waterford is 400 years old.

After Seaton there is a tarmac path leading through more dunes, again running more or less parallel with the road and the sea, as far as the golfing links at **Blyth Beach**. At the Coastline Fish & Chip restaurant you should turn left, cross over the main road and follow the cycle-way around Blyth.

Coastline Fish and Chips – *a no frills setting for fine fresh battered cod and haddock. For £5.00 you get enough to feed a small village, and a pot of tea to wash it down. Worth stopping off, but don't expect a fast getaway.*

For the next section of the journey you need to keep your wits about you, due to some poor signposting and a bewildering number of path options. First you head 1km up the A1061 towards **Cramlington**, before crossing the road. You will soon see a curved sign indicating a left turn painted on the pathway – don't take the immediate sharp left, as would seem the obvious choice; take the middle of three paths to the right of a blue cycle sign **(map p.135)**.

Ten yards on you see a Route 1 sign, which takes you through some houses, to the end of Barras Avenue. Cross over Plessey Road and pick up a blue sign opposite, going

Seaton Sluice Harbour

right into Newlands Ave. Continue for 400 metres and head left into Fifteenth Ave, then left into Sixth Ave. At the crossroads with Eighth Ave, go across into Twentieth Ave, then right after 60m, up an alley. At the end, go right then first left, into Southend Ave.

Go past the Isabella pub to the end of the road and turn right past the back of a terrace of new houses. Go left at the end into Cowpen and Newsham, keeping four cooling towers to your right, then go over a bridge, over the disused railway. Pay attention here! Over the bridge there is a cycle path to the left, and just further on, one to the right – and confusingly – one also taking a middle course. Take the middle one, and after 200m or so, your decision will be rewarded by the sight of a blue sign confirming that you are *en route*.

You are on Tynedale Dve – proceed to the end and take a sharp left by a playing field. If you can see Tynedale Place, you've gone too far. Keep going as far as the traffic island and hang a right past some new houses. Cross the road and take the cycle lane past Asda. Congratulations! You have made it past the labyrinthine and sporadically signposted suburbs of **Blyth**. The best bit of Blyth is the old town, by the marina and harbour. See the map if you fancy taking the diversion.

Getting through **Bedlington Station** and **East Sleekburn** is easy. Keep peddling; you will soon be out of this seemingly unremitting landscape of industrial heritage. The track follows the A189 for four or five kilometres, taking the middle course between **Ashington** and **Newbiggin-by-the-Sea**. If you want to stop in **Newbiggin**, take the B1334 – 1km after crossing the River Wansbeck – into the centre.

St Mary's lighthouse, Whitley Bay

Newbiggin is built around a crescent-shaped bay, protected by two rocky bluffs. It is popular with sailors and golfers. Not a huge amount seems to have happened here between the Viking invasion in 875AD (when the town's name changed from South Wallerick to Neubegang) and John Braine penning Room at the Top whilst working as a librarian in the 1950s. A still point in a turning world, clearly.

If you're bypassing Newbiggin, continue past **Woodburn** and the giant aluminium works, the power stations and proceed into **Lynemouth**. If you're overnighting in Newbiggin, retrace your steps up the B1334, or chance it on the more direct but much busier A197, which links up with the route at Woodburn.

ACCOMMODATION

SEATON HOUSE
Mary & Robert Dodds,
Seaton Avenue,
Newbiggin-by-the-Sea,
NE64 6UX
T:+44 (0)1670 816057
Rooms: 2 singles, 1 double, 1 twin
B&B: £19 to £20
Evening meals: No – complimentary snacks. Eating places and pubs 100m.
Packed lunch: £3
Smoking: Yes – in seated garden area
Distance from C&C: On route
3 Diamonds
Relaxed, homely atmosphere. Tea, hot showers, drying facilities, secure cycle storage – popular with cyclists, walkers and tourists. Two minutes from seafront. Good breakfasts and caters for vegetarians.

Overleaf: first taste of coastal Northumberland - Druridge Bay

Just a couple of kilometres up the road, the **Lynemouth Community Trust** *at the* **Lynemouth Resource Centre** *in Bridge Rd. provides another handy stop-off point for the* weary. Café, toilets, cycle parking, local info and basic cycle spares and free internet. **(see ad on p.128)** *You will be cycling past its front door.*

The route now heads from urban to rural as you hit the coastline near **Snab Point** and **Cresswell**. Here you can eat well at the **Drifters Cafe Restaurant** opposite the beach. There is very little in the way of amenities until **Amble**, some 18km north of Lynemouth. You are now on the edge of the Druridge Bay nature reserve, a large, sweeping sand and shingle bay *(see p.30-31)*. This area has been inhabited since the Stone Age, when the forests were cleared and the dunes used for cattle grazing.

There are rock pools at low tide and sand dunes marking a natural barrier between land and sea. This is your first taste of typical Northumberland coastline.

Amble marks another (brief) urban interlude. Positioned on the mouth of the River Coquet, Amble is Northumberland's most important fishing port north of the Tyne, and was originally a prehistoric settlement. There is evidence that the Romans too lived here before the Benedictine monks arrived in the 11th century. The coal industry in the 19th century led to its expansion.

Now there's a 200-berth marina and trips to Coquet Island bird sanctuary run regularly in May and June. **Tourist Information Centre: T:**+44 (0)1665 712313.

There's also **Breeze Bikes—** *small and extremely helpful outfit run by Mark Breeze. He also has a recovery service for those in serious trouble and will even lend out bikes if repairs look like taking a long time.* **Coquet Garage**, *Coquet Street, NE65.* **T:***+44 (0)1665 710323.*

Coming out of Amble take the cycle path along the A1068 for 2km up to Warkworth. It is more direct than the Sustrans alternative, and follows the estuary.

WARKWORTH

North view of Warkworth castle from the coastal track

WARKWORTH. At the top of the hill, take a right. Round the bend you see the castle. Those not rushing should take the time to visit – it is arguably the most splendid ruin of its type in Northumbria. Largely intact, it has retained its original character thanks to not being heavily restored. Originally built in 1139, the main sections of the castle were constructed in the late 14th century. The castle, which completely dominates Warkworth, was in the hands of the Percy family for more than 600 years until given to the Crown in 1922.

The jewel amongst English Heritage's northern castles, architecturally it is a mixed bag: every century, from the 12th onwards, bears its imprimatur. Along with Alnwick castle, it was home to the Percy family, and Harry Hotspur, the first Earl of Northumberland's son, who was killed at the Battle of Shrewsbury in 1403. It is also Shakespeare's setting for Henry IV, Part II. It also has a 5-star lock-up, with its own window, fireplace, cupboards and WC, clearly built for Very Important Prisoners.

Warkworth has plenty of pubs and eateries, and is a charming village bottled into a loop in the river Coquet. Notwithstanding the posh prison, the best place to stay now is the Sun Hotel, directly opposite the Castle.

ACCOMMODATION

SUN HOTEL
Joanne and Anthony Middlemas,
6 Castle Terrace,
Warkworth
NE 65 0UP
T:+44 (0)1665 711259 **F:**+44 (0)1665 711833
Rooms: 6 twins, 6 doubles and 2 family.
B&B: From £44 for a single to £65 for two sharing twins.
Evening meal: From £5.99 to £15
Packed lunch: From £5
Northumbria Tourist Board **2-stars**.

The hotel was built in the 17th century and is opposite the dramatic ruins of the castle. The conservatory offers spectacular views of the river and sea, and there's a superb choice of bar meals at lunch time and in the evening. Plenty of lock-up space for bikes.

Down Castle Street (the main thoroughfare) is the **Masons Arms**, *a pub with excellent food run by chef David Race. Serves lunches 12-2 and dinners 6-9 (7-9 on Sundays). Restaurant-style food served in an informal atmosphere. Full Sunday roasts available 12-2, and daily specials incorporating local produce including fish and seafood. There's a constantly changing range of cask ale and a large walled beer garden with access to idyllic riverside walks* **T:**+44 (0)1665 711398

To leave town you cross the river Coquet. Watch out for a sharp right, signposted for the beach and cemetery. You can take this turn, or go left slightly further up the road, following a longer route through the lanes into Alnmouth.

I prefer the former, as it is coastal and more scenic. Make sure you stop and look back at the castle as you go up the hill. This is the best vantage point for this formidable bastion; on seeing this, marauders from the north must have thought twice before advancing. The whole village is laid out before you with its teashops, pubs and hotels all bottled into the tightly packed peninsula created by the river. This is the best view of Warkworth, the place to shoot your pictures.

At the top of the hill you head left onto a track which shortly brings you back to the edge of the A1068. After 100m it veers right. Follow the cycle signs for **Alnmouth**, the next settlement up the coast.

The sea appears behind a wooden footbridge, slapping around the base of the Birling Carrs rocks, a grand, grey and deeply uninviting expanse until the sun comes out. To the right a distant lighthouse looms above the rocky Amble shore. You then pass through a patch of beach devoted to a discreet but slightly shabby caravan park, which thankfully merges tastefully into the sandy undulations.

Alnmouth beach viewed from the dunes by the golf course

Through a rickety gate are the **Alnmouth Dunes**, protected, like the rest of the coast between Seahouses and Druridge Bay, by the National Trust. The route is rough and steep before it turns 90 degrees inland up a stone-strewn path.

After a 1km climb, follow the long slope to the outskirts of Alnmouth, with its picture-postcard pastel cottages and red pantiled 18th century roofs. This little town is also on a peninsula created by the river on one side, and the sea and sand to the east.

A former smuggler's den on the end of the Aln estuary, Alnmouth is now a yachty haven and boasts one of Britain's oldest golf courses and splendid walks up to Foxton Hall and Seaton Point.

There are beautiful beach walks. Church Hill is the site of an Anglo-Saxon church. A huge storm on Christmas Day 1806 led to the river bursting its banks and forever changing direction, pouring out into the sea through a new opening to the north of Church Hill, leaving the old harbour redundant and silted.

ACCOMMODATION

THE BEACHES
Susan and Donald Hall,
Northumberland St,
Alnmouth, NE66 2RS
T:+44 (0)1665 830443
E: le.chef@breathe.com **W:** www.beachesbyo.co.uk
Rooms: 3 from: £30
Evening meal: From £10 for 3 courses.
Packed lunch: Yes.
Smoking: Only in communal room.
Distance from C&C: Just 100m or so from the route.
Bike store and clothes drying. Right by the pubs and restaurants.
Fun place. Evening meals are informal, cheap and friendly in
intimate surroundings. Ships' lanterns flicker, nets are draped
over the ceiling, charts bedeck the walls and salt is in the air.
Steak and lobster for around than £15! BYOB (Bring Your
Own Bottle). Party time!

HOPE AND ANCHOR
Debbie and George Philipson,
44 Northumberland St,
Alnmouth,
NE44 2RA
T:+44 (0)1665 830363
F:+44 (0)1665 603082
E: debbiephilipson@hopeandanchorholidays.ssnet.co.uk
W: www.hopeandanchorholidays.co.uk
Rooms: 4 doubles, 1 twin, 3 family. From £32 to£40 for single.
Evening meal: From approx. £10 to £15.
Packed lunch: From £4.50
Smoking: Downstairs only.
Cosy coastal inn renowned for its friendly atmosphere and
good home cooking. Beautiful beaches, golf, walking and
cycling plus bike lock-up and drying facilities. Fine selection of
malt whiskies and cask conditioned ale.

BILTON BARNS FARMHOUSE

Dorothy Jackson,
Bilton Barns,
Alnmouth,
Alnwick,
NE66 2TB
T:+44 (0)1665 830427
E: dorothy@biltonbarns.co.uk
Rooms: 1 single, 3 doubles, 3 twins, 1 family.
Rates: £26 to £32
Evening meal: £15
Packed lunch: £5
Smoking: No.
Distance from Coast & Castles: 2.5km (just outside Alnmouth, on the B1388 beyond the railway station. It is down a farm track on the left, opposite Spy Law).
4 diamonds plus **Silver Award** ETC.
Distance from pubs and restaurants: 2.5km
Farmhouse B&B with converted granaries as suites. All rooms are en-suite, beautifully furnished and have magnificent views across Alnmouth bay. Self-catering cottages also available.

Both Alnmouth and Warkworth are perfectly preserved period pieces. They are unlikely to change radically in character because they are circumscribed by water, hemmed into their peninsulas with no room to expand.

Indeed the entire Northumberland coast north of Blyth seems timeless. From Alnmouth, go up to the island at the edge of the village and take the second exit, the one beyond the road you came in on. After 1km you fork right towards Boulmer.

At **Boulmer** you can take the longer original Sustrans route past the RAF station and **Longhoughton** by following the lane round to the left, or you can take the rough track along the coast, which is also signposted. This is far more worthwhile if you are not in a rush; there are gates, but there are some beautiful views of the pink-tinged sands. When the tide is out the whelkers, winkle and mussel pickers go to work, and the sweet smell of seaweed and salt, ozone and seaspray fill the air. As you resume the path from the beach at **Howdiemont Sands**, the smell of cattle takes over.

The track ends and an old, little-used road begins, taking you to Craster South Farm. Here you fork right towards **Craster** and **Dunstan**, past the 15th century **Craster Tower** where the Craster family, who have been associated with this corner for nearly 1,000 years, live.

Craster is another must if you can afford the time.

*Here at the **Jolly Fisherman**, you can sample the fabled fresh crab soup (the recipe is a national secret), kipper pate or various freshly made sandwiches and golden chips fried in dripping.*
***T:**+44 (0)1665 576218*
The pub has featured on TV and in newspapers. The dining room overlooks the pretty harbour.

Look north and see the craggy remains of **Dunstanburgh Castle**, once the home of John of Gaunt. The epitome of what a real ruin should look like.

If you want to mail home a pungent memory of the trip, try the famous 100 year old Craster smokery, L.Robson & Sons. Arguably the best kippers (smoked herring) in Britain, they also sell crabs and lobsters harvested from the nearby whinstone platform.
***W:** www.kipper.co.uk **T:**+44 (0) 01665 576223 or **F:**+44 (0)1665 576044).*

HOWICK SCAR FARM HOUSE

Celia Curry, Craster, Alnwick, NE66 3SU
T/F: 01665 576665
E: howick.scar@virgin.net **W:** www.howickscar.co.uk
Rooms: 2 - 2 dbls **B&B:** £20-£28
Evening meal: pub in Dunstan (1km) or Craster (1.5km).
Packed lunch: no **Smoking:** no
3-diamonds ETC. Cosy farmhouse setting in wild and
windy Northumberland. Rooms have sea views. Tea & coffee
facilities, bathrobes, secure storage and drying. Charming spot.

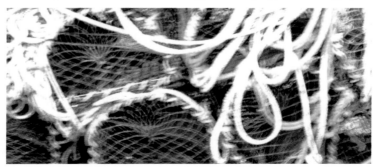

To get back on the route, go up the hill and turn right, passing the caravan park at Proctor's Stead. Here you take another right down to Dunstan Square, where a 2.5km track takes you across to **Dunstan Steads**. Take time to admire the great view of the castle to your right. Once at the Steads, go left to **Embleton**.

There are a handful of watering holes and places to stay in this bijou village.

THE SPORTSMAN
Manager: James Chorlton,
Sea Lane,
Embleton,
Alnwick,
NE 66 3XF
T:+44 (0)1665 576588
F:+44 (0)1665 576524
W: www.sportsmanhotel.co.uk

Rooms: 11 en-suite (3 dbl, 2 twin, 4 family)
B&B: £26 to £30
Evening meal: £5.95 to £12.95
Packed lunch: £3.50 to £4.50
Smoking: In designated areas only.
Drying and **washing** facilities.
Pubs & restaurants on doorstep.
ETC **3-diamond**

Manager James is a real bikey. He's got links with Breeze Bikes in Amble to do technical services, repairs and sell spares. The hotel has great views of Dunstanburgh Castle and Embleton Bay. Discounts for group bookings!

1km or so beyond the village you get to the B1340. Here, there is a choice: left past **Christon Bank**, **Preston**, **Chathill**, **West Fleetham** and meander all the way to **Bamburgh** via **North Sunderland**, or right – the way I would advise. This takes you down to a T-junction, where you can go left and proceed northwards (NB don't go right down the B1339 as this would take you full circle back to Embleton). Or go straight on down the lane that leads to High Newton-by-the-Sea.

When you get to High Newton, carry on until the road bears round to the right for **Low Newton**. This is basically a three-sided square (Embleton Bay provides the fourth) comprising Georgian period dwellings and the **Ship Inn**.

*At the northern tip of Embleton Bay, the **Ship** dates from 1790. It is just metres from the sea, serves real ale and food, and there is a flat that will sleep 4 for £55 a night (speak to landlady Christine Forsyth **T:**+44 (0)1665 576262).*

The view from Embleton Bay

It is part of a National Trust owned village square, and is car-free, and what's more it is in the Good Beer Guide. Beyond the sand dunes is Newton Pool Nature Reserve with bird hides where you can watch any number of feathered exotica.

Back on the B1340, head northwards towards Swinhoe (right if coming back from Newton, left if coming from Christon Bank). At **Swinhoe**, hang a right to **Beadnell**. This place is well worth the detour, especially to watch the sun setting

Sunset on the East coast? Why Beadnell is unique

over the the water. You may wonder how this can be, given that you are travelling along the east coast! However Beadnell Harbour is on a south-facing peninsula, so you can look west across the water with spectacular results; indeed, it is the only harbour on England's east coast to face west. There are also 18th century lime kilns near the dunes.

ACCOMMODATION

BEACH COURT

Harbour Road,
Beadnell,
NE67 5BJ
T:+44 (0)1665 720225
F:+44 (0)1665 721499
E: info@beachcourt.com
W: www.beachcourt.com
Rooms: 3 double bedrooms.
B&B: From £44.50 pp. Cheviot suite £119 for two.
Distance from C&C: 3km diversion.
Pubs and restaurants within walking distance.
Five diamonds: Right on the shore adjacent to the 18th century harbour. Stone-built turreted bastion with individual suites, plus oak panelled sea-facing drawing room, dining room and conservatory. Walled courtyard and miles of sand.

Follow the lane back up to B1340, then continue along the coast to **Seahouses**. This is a haven for fish and chip lovers. It's also handy if you need to stock up on victuals. The harbour is imposing and handsome, a 19th century relic of the once-profitable herring industry. Nowadays yachts share berths with the remaining fishing fleet and there are boat trips to the Farne Islands. There are 28 volcanic outcrops 2-5 miles off the coast; they contain a huge variety of seabirds, not to mention one of Europe's most important colonies of rare grey seals — the largest surviving carnivores in the British Isles. Two of Britain's most important early Christian leaders, St Cuthbert and St Aidan, used to visit them to meditate.

*A great place for a pint and some lunch or dinner is the **OLDE SHIP HOTEL**, overlooking the harbour. Run by Alan and Jean Glen, it has been in the same family for nearly a century. A cornucopia of maritime salvage, a living museum and a time capsule, the Ship has a*

truly great bar – blazing coal fire, polished brass and fine ales. The food is wholesome and good value, and the rooms (from £39pp) are very comfortable. There are also adjoining apartments and suites. However the hotel is not suited to big parties or children, so bear this in mind.

T:+44 (0)1665 720200
W: www.seahouses.co.uk or theoldeship@seahouses.co.uk). AA, RAC & ETB 2-star.

THE LODGE at 146 Main Street, Seahouses (NE68 7UA), provides modestly priced accommodation.
T:+44 (0)1665 720158
E: thelodge@hotmail.com
Rooms: 5 plus one with 2 singles plus bunks.
B&B: £22 to £26
Bar with pool table providing dinner from £4.95 to £14.95
Distance from C&C: On route.
Fisherman Andrew Douglas who runs this cosy pine bar with 'indoor aquarium' and chalet-style bedrooms all on one level, with en-suite facilities. There is a lock-up for bikes and an informal atmosphere.

THE LINKS HOTEL
Malcolm Sutton and Julie Dawson,
8 King St,.
Seahouses,
NE 68 7XP
T:+44 (0)1665 720062 **F:**+44 (0)1665 720958
Rooms: 4 double, 4 twins and 2 family.

B&B: £26 to £32
Evening meal: From £4.95 to £17.95
Packed lunch: Yes – price dependent upon request
Smoking: Yes
Distance from C&C: Just metres from route.

AA **2-star**: Two minutes' walk from the harbour and golf courses. 'Excellent food endorsed by the numbers of guests returning year after year.' Ideal base for discovering Northumbria.

LONGSTONE HOUSE HOTEL

Trevor & Anne Leadbitter,
182 Main St,
Seahouses,
NE68 7UA
T: +44 (0)1665 720212
F: +44 (0)1665 720211
E: info@longstonehousehotel.co.uk
W: www.longstonehousehotel.co.uk
Rooms: 17 en-suite.
B&B: From £25 to £34
Packed lunch: From £3
Evening meal: From £5.95 to £14.95

"A family run, licensed hotel with a reputation for fine food and ale. We are cyclist-friendly, with secure stores for bicycles by prior arrangement. A warm welcome awaits all our guests," says Trevor.
(see ad on p.128)

Right: Seahouses lighthouse

Left: The harbour and the Olde Ship.

BAMBURGH

The most obvious way – and far the prettiest – to get to **Bamburgh** from Seahouses is the 5km stretch along the B1340 coastal road. Sustrans recommends an inland alternative which heads west through North Sunderland, past West Field Farm. It is well sign-posted, slightly longer and does avoid traffic, which can be hectic in the summer.

From the coastal road you get a good view across the Inner Sound to the Farne Islands, beyond St Aidan's Dunes. This magnificent 25-mile coastal sweep of virtually non-stop sand reaches way beyond **Budle Bay** and **Holy Island**, almost as far north as **Berwick**, and as far south as **Embleton Bay**.

Bamburgh is a quaint village stretching up the hill from the massively imposing castle. It is also the ancient capital of Northumbria, settled by the Saxon monarch Ida, the 5th century founder of the kingdom. It was once known as 'Bebbanburgh', after Bebba, the wife of Ida's grandson.

Christianity came in the 7th century, and in 635AD King Oswald and St Aidan built the kingdom's first church, probably on the site of the 800 year-old church which still stands in Bamburgh. The castle was frequently razed by Vikings. Rebuilt in the 11th century, it was significantly reconstructed in 1272

It subsequently fell into disrepair. In 1704 Lord Crewe, the last of the Prince Bishops of Durham, bought the castle and founded a charity school for girls. It must have been a cold and windy establishment, a breeder of tough women. Financial difficulties led to it being sold as a private home in 1894 to William, 1st Lord Armstrong, who restored it to its present magnificence. The Armstrong family is still in residence,

Grace Darling, Northumbria's most famous heroine, is buried in Bamburgh. She kept the Longstone Lighthouse on the Farne Islands, and is remembered for rowing into a foul storm to rescue passengers on a rock-impaled Dundee-bound steamship, the Forfarshire, in 1838.

Bamburgh village seen from the castle

Bamburgh Castle seen from the village

BAMBURGH - "GREENGATES"

Claire Sundin,
34, Front St, Bamburgh, NE69 7BJ
T:+44 (0)1668 214535
E:greengatesbamburgh@amserve.com
Rooms: 1 double, 2 twin.
B&B: From £25
Packed lunch: on request
On route. Pubs and restaurants on the doorstep, and only 100M from the castle. "Serving all local produce to provide exceptional pedal power for your day ahead," says Claire.

There are more direct ways of getting from Newcastle to this part of Northumbria, as the road sign near Bamburgh makes clear: Newcastle 48 Miles (77km), it says. Do not be put off! My trip clock, with all the fascinating diversions, read 84.36miles (135km)! There are two ways to get from Bamburgh to **Belford**. The first, which goes to **Waren Mill** (*see accommodation below*) by way of **Budle Bay** along the B1342, is the more attractive, though traffic in the summer might make the Sustrans alternative along the B1341 a better bet. If you follow the former route, take the road to the right when you get to Waren Mill. You soon see the Route 1 signs.

If you take the latter, the Mizen Head Hotel should be on your right as you leave Bamburgh. Be careful coming out of Spindlestone, just past the weir; the road is steep and uneven. I came off, thanks to thick farm mud covering a rut. It was only the quick reactions of the driver behind me that saved my head being spread across the road.

Go right at the windmill, passing Chesterhill Farm, then go left all the way to the level crossing. You then have to cross the A1 on a fast and dangerous stretch before the steep climb up to Belford. At the top of the hill go right, or take a left down the hill into Belford.

BUDLE BAY CAMP SITE

Mrs Phyl Carruthers,
Waren Mill,
Nr Bamburgh,
NE 70 7EE
T: +44 (0)1668 214598
E: phyl.carruthers@virgin.net

250 pitches for tourers and tents – seasonal touring pitches available for those wishing to base themselves here. Electric hook up, showers, toilets, laundrette, snack bar. Nearest pubs and restaurants in Bamburgh or Belford, both 5km.

Opposite: Bird throngs on the Farne Islands, just off Bamburgh

Pitch: £5.50 for 1 with small tent; £9.00 sharing.
Evening meal: Yes – £3.50.
Packed lunch: Yes – £2.50.
One of the most beautiful sites on the Northumberland coast. Lots of wildlife, canoeing, diving and walking.

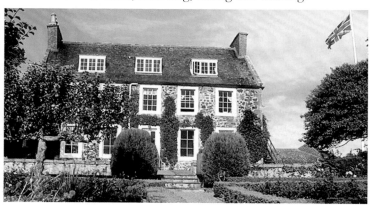

WAREN HOUSE HOTEL

Peter & Anita Laverack,
Waren Mill, Nr Bamburgh,
NE70 7EE
T: +44 (0)1668 214581 **F:** +44 (0)1668 214484
E: enquiries@warenhousehotel.co.uk
W: www.warenhousehotel.co.uk
Rooms: 4 double, 3 twins, 4 suites.
B&B: from £42 to £97.50
Packed lunch: From £5.50
Evening meal: From £22 to £27.50. Last orders 20.30.
Smoking: No, except in library.
Nearest pub and restaurant: 3 miles
AA/RAC/ETC **3-star**. Johansen's Recommended.
Traditional country house hotel on the edge of Budle Bay, three miles west of Bamburgh and 14 miles south of Berwick. Superb accommodation, excellent food and fine wine. Just take a look at the website!

DETCHANT FARM
Brenda Jackson,
Belford,
NE70 7PF
T:+44 (0)1668 213261 **F:**+44 (0)1668 219261
E: detchant@farming.co.uk
Rooms: 1 twin.
B&B: £22.50 to £25
Packed lunch: £5
Smoking: No.
Distance from pubs and restaurants: 2 miles
ETC **3 diamonds**
This is a family run farm situated between the coast and the Cheviot Hills just two miles north of Belford. The route runs past the front door, and the room itself looks across at **Lindisfarne** (Holy Island). An ideal place for anyone wishing to explore the area.

THE FARMHOUSE GUEST HOUSE
Carol Wood, 24 West St, Belford, NE70 7QE
T:+44 (0)1668 213083
Rooms: 2 doubles (1 en-suite, 1 with private facilities), 1 family with 3 single beds (en-suite).
B&B: £19 to £23 (£5 surcharge for single occupancy).
Packed lunch: £3 to £4 **Smoking:** No.
Pubs and restaurants: On doorstep
Distance from C&C: 0.5km.
ETC **4 diamonds:** Small, comfortable village location. Excellent breakfasts. Guest lounge with coal and log fires and good drying facilities.

Previous page: Belford village centre, just 0.5 km from the route

BLACK SWAN HOTEL

Jim Bryson & Marie Silk
Cragside Avenue
Belford NE70
T: 01668 213266
Rooms: 2 - 1 twin, 1 dbl
B&B: £45 per room; single £25-£40 (seasonal)
Evening meal: £6.95 to £11.95
Packed lunch: Yes. Depends what you have.
Smoking: Yes
Distance from C&C: 0.5km

Busy village inn serving some good real ale and robust home-cooked fare. This is a good, no-nonsense, traditional village inn - one of six servicing a local population of 1,200.

The route from Belford to **Fenwick** runs almost parallel with the A1 before crossing at West Mains, near the Plough Hotel. If you are going to take the five mile detour to Holy Island (there are NO excuses for not doing so unless you are competing in a race!) you cross the railway line once again, and take the causeway. But first, check the tide times by calling the Holy Island postmaster, Malcolm Patterson (01289 389271). There is also a tide table on the causeway.

Holy Island - castle and ruined Priory (below)

HOLY ISLAND

HISTORICAL NOTE:

In 635AD St Aidan walked across the vast sandbank, along what is now known as Pilgrim's Way, and founded a monastery that was to become the spiritual and educational heart of Northumbria. Originally known as Lindisfarne, Holy Island was also the home of St Cuthbert, the reclusive missionary who sought solace in solitude. The seminal influence of Cuthbert and Aidan made the kingdom arguably the most enlightened part of Europe during the 7th, 8th and 9th centuries. Bishop Eidfrith (Abbot of Lindisfarne from 698-721) produced the Lindisfarne Gospels, the fabled and magnificent manuscripts created around 700AD to commemorate the life of St Cuthbert.

This period of peace, poetry, monumental carving and saints was known as the 'Golden Age' of Northumbria preceding, as it did, the bloody arrival of the Vikings in 793. A century later, after repeated attacks, they were forced to flee, carrying the body of St Cuthbert and all the holy relics they could manage. They did not return until just after the Norman Conquest, when the Benedictines rebuilt the magnificent priory and renamed it Holy Island. For 500 years the priory functioned, until Henry VIII ordered the Dissolution of the Monasteries during the Reformation.

The castle was built to defend the island from the Scots. During the Civil War it was a Royalist stronghold, before falling to the Parliamentarians. Restored to full baronial splendour exactly a century ago by Sir Edwin Lutyens, the architect of the Houses of Parliament, it now belongs to the National Trust. Twice a day the cradle of British Christianity is cut off by the tide, restoring peace and tranquillity from the hordes of tourists. If you want to spend the night here you MUST book in advance. There are not many beds on the island and demand for them is VERY high.

CROWN & ANCHOR INN

David Foxton *(pictured above)*,
Holy Island,
Berwick-upon-Tweed,
TD15 2RR
T:+44 (0)1289 389215 **F:**+44 (0)1289 389041
E: crownandanchorinn@fsnet.co.uk
W: www.crownandanchorinn.co.uk
Rooms: 3 – 2 double, 1 twin. Single occupancy: £40,
double £70
Packed lunch: £5.50
Dinner: £18
Lunch: £5 to £7
Smoking: Bar only.

This is a restaurant with rooms (and a busy bar). The focus is on food, and the menu changes daily. Foxton, the chef-proprietor, specialises in locally sourced produce and the results are well worth the detour onto the island. The rooms command wonderful views. Book well in advance.

LINDISFARNE HERITAGE CENTRE (Marygate, Holy Island, **T:**+44 (0)1289 389004) is a wonderful information and exhibition centre run by the people of Holy Island. Among the works on display are the Lindisfarne Gospels computer interactive exhibition (the real Gospels are safely stored at the British Library) portraying the story, creation and contents of this masterpiece of early medieval art. You can even lug home a facsimile if there's room in your pannier. Admission £2.50 all year round. Well worth a visit.

It would be hard to miss the Priory, despite the best efforts of Henry Tudor. This site is maintained by English Heritage, who charge £3.00 to let you in and mooch about. They also look after several other wonderful sites on the English side of the route: Dunstanburgh Castle (£1.90), Warkworth Castle (£2.60), the Barracks at Berwick-upon-Tweed (£2.80) and Norham Castle (£2.80). Their visitor centre on Holy Island **T:**+44 (0)1289 330733 is also worth a visit, even if you don't actually feel like paying to go inside the Priory next door.

Beachcomber campsite overlooks Holy Island

After the causeway, go through **Beal** before turning right immediately after crossing the railway line. The path is often muddy and continues for 2km before you re-cross the line. This takes you down to **Goswick**, to the edge of the vast Goswick Sands, which thrust out into the sea as far across as Holy Island.

If you fancy a night under canvas, nestling amongst the dunes, **BEACHCOMBER CAMPSITE**, Goswick, TD15 2RW, provides a fairly perfect setting. Former schoolmaster John Gregson runs this friendly establishment.

T: +44 (0)1289 381217
E: johngregson@micro-plus-web.net
50 pitches
Cost per night: £3.50 to £5
Evening meals: 7-9pm
Drying facilities: Yes.

There is a bar and eating area just 20m from the site, and the route is 400m away.

ETC **3-star**

Situated behind the dunes of the beach, Beachcomber overlooks Holy Island and is the nearest campsite to the tourist Mecca. Hot showers – all equipment included in per person charge. Horse riding on site.

If you don't fancy a night under canvas, then head left at the end of the track by the cottages, and head along the track through the golf course. Hang a left, take care on the level crossing and you will soon find yourself passing the tiny hamlet of **Cheswick**. Just before you get there you will see a magnificent Georgian house up a drive to your left. This is Ladythorne Guest House *(see below - details overleaf)*.

LADYTHORNE HOUSE

Val Parker,
Cheswick,
Berwick,
TD15 2RW
T: +44 (0)1289 387382 **F:** +44 (0)1289 387073
E: valparker@ladythorneguesthouse.freeserve.co.uk
Rooms: 6 -- 1 double, 1 single, 2 twin and 2 family.
B&B: £17 to £19
Evening meals: No. **Packed lunch:** £4
Smoking: No. **Nearest pub/eating place:** 2km
ETC **3-diamond.**

This country house was built in 1721 and restored by the Parkers. The scenery is beautiful and ideal for touring north Northumberland. Holy Island is 13km.

You now head back to the coast, through **Cocklawburn Nature Reserve** *(below)* above the last of the great Northumbrian sand dunes. Rare plants flourish along this stretch and in the spring it is ablaze with colour. It is also home to one of the biggest colonies of grayling butterflies in the country.

BERWICK-UPON-TWEED

Berwick 'Royal Border' rail bridge over the Tweed

Once beyond the reserve you find yourself sandwiched between the fast rail line and the cliff, on a muddy track that the local farmer's cattle cannot fail to turn into a quagmire in the rain. There's just over 2km of this - and it can be very hard work - before you descend into Spittal, on the outskirts of Berwick **(map p.135)**.

Follow the road through **Tweedmouth** and past the dock area, and then either: 1) cross the old bridge pushing your bike (it's one-way), into the town itself (this brings you into the Quay Wall area, and the fascinating lower ramparts).

Or: 2) carry on round the Route 1 sign-posted system and over the higher, newer bridge, which takes you – sharp left – along the river and up Tweed St, past the station.

But stop, get your breath. Take a look. Spend a night, if you can! There are lots of places to stay.

BERWICK is a fine, handsome and once very wealthy town. It has good pubs, a few restaurants and bags of character. Steeped in blood-soaked history, and fascinating to explore, it is built upon a peninsula at the mouth of the Tweed. Historically a commercial town, it faces the river, rather than the sea. Three bridges connect it with Tweedmouth on the south side of the estuary: the low stone bridge with 15 arches of varying height and width, completed in 1634; the 1928 concrete span known as the 'Royal Tweed,' and the railway's 'Royal Border', with its 28 soaring arches, completed in 1850. The town is best seen from the Tweedmouth bank or the railway bridge. Tweedmouth itself holds a feast on the Sunday after 18th July honouring St Boisil, a Saxon holy Man to whom the present St Bartholomew's Church was dedicated at its founding in 1143. Today the 'Salmon Queen's' coronation opens a week of events (well worth coinciding with).

Berwick sits on the north bank of the Tweed, at the east end of the long disputed border. It changed hands no fewer than 13 times until finally being snatched from Scotland by Richard III in 1482. The fortifications, started in 1558, make it one of Europe's most outstanding fortified towns.

Coxons Tower, part of the fine Elizabethan battlements.

And so it should be; the staggering cost of nearly £130,000 constituted the single most expensive undertaking of the Elizabethan period. The defensive walls were built centuries earlier, during the reign of Edward II.

The barracks were constructed in 1717 in response to the first uprising by the Scottish Jacobites in 1715, and bear witness to the strategic importance of the frontier. Long before that, Berwick was a prosperous and occasionally peaceful Scottish 'burgh', having enjoyed a golden age during the 12th and 13th centuries, when it was a centre of European commerce, and had its own mint and royal castle.

This came to a spectacularly bloody end, when the area became so warlike that the monks on Holy Island spent more money on gunpowder than they did on parchment. The

Scottish border, which had once reached as far south as Hull, changed radically once again. Lands were grabbed back in 1174, along with strategic castles at Berwick, Roxburgh and Edinburgh.

However Richard the Lionheart soon sold them back to the Scots to finance his crusades, but cross-border conflict rumbled on.

Unspoilt Berwick: Palace Green

Edward I, 'Hammer of the Scots', decided to sort matters out once and for all by raiding and sacking Berwick on March 30, 1296. And 'by his gracious power killed 25,700 people', including all the Flemish and German wool and wine merchants who had helped build the town's prosperity. To further stamp their authority, the English then displayed one quarter of the corpse of William Wallace (Braveheart) on a pike after he was executed in London in 1305. One assumes that Wallace Green was named after him. Berwick was, in terms of tax revenue, the fourth most important town in England by 1300. That is why it was so fought over. Robert the Bruce reclaimed it after Bannockburn in 1314 and it remained Scottish until 1333, after which the to-ing and fro-ing became such that, on occasions, both sides occupied different parts of the town at the same time.

There is some urban myth as well. Berwick was granted a special status as a free borough in 1502, and was mentioned separately in Acts of Parliament. Berwick was 'of', but not 'within' the Kingdom of England, thus documents were signed by England, Wales and Berwick-upon-Tweed. For this reason it was supposed still to be at war with Russia in the Crimea, having been specifically listed as declaring hostilities in 1854, but having been missed off the ensuing peace treaty two years later. This alarming state of affairs, though not supported by any historical evidence, was not resolved until the 1960s, when Khrushchev sent an emissary to the north east to formally end the war. Current thinking suggests that this urban myth was perpetrated a century ago by a local Archdeacon with a sense of fun.

A tour of the Barracks and the museum gives a wonderful insight, not only into regimental history, but also the town's schizophrenic past. Originally home to the 25th Regiment of Foot, it was used as a staging post on the journey north, and became home to the King's Own Scottish Borderers in the 1880s. It is still their regimental headquarters. After seeing this, a two mile walk around the ramparts, perhaps taking in one or two of the pubs, is a must, even for tired cyclists!

ACCOMMODATION

CASTLE HOTEL
Donald Ringland, 103 Castlegate, Berwick, TD15 1LF
T:+44 (0)1289 307900
E: ringers.home@virgin.net
Rooms: 16 – 3 single, 7 double, 5 twin, 1 family.
B&B: £27 to £42
Packed lunch: Prior arrangement. **Evening meal:** On request - from £7.50 to £15. **Smoking:** Yes in most areas.
ETC: **3 diamonds**: The Castle offers comfort, convenience and care at affordable prices. Large or small parties catered for. Next to Berwick railway station, it is the perfect base for exploring North Northumberland and the Scottish Borders.

CLOVELLY HOUSE
Viv Lawrence, 58 West St, Berwick, TD15 1AS
T:+44 (0)1289 302337 **F:**+44 (0)1289 302052
E: vivroc@clovelly53.freeserve.co.uk
Rooms: 3 – 1 single, 1 double, 1 twin or family.
B&B: £19 to £25. **Evening meals:** No.
Packed lunch: £3 to £5. **Smoking:** In designated area.
Drying facilities: Yes. ETC **4-diamonds** and **silver award**
Centrally situated, close to the bars and restaurants and other amenities. "You'll get a warm welcome to our quality home," says Viv. You'll also get a monster breakfast.

MEADOW HILL GUEST HOUSE
Barry & Hazel Hill, Duns Rd, Berwick, TD15 1UB
T & F: +44 (0)1289 306325
E: barryandhazel@meadow-hill.co.uk
W: www.meadow-hill.co.uk
Rooms: 4 – 1 dbl or single, 1 twin, 2 multipurpose (i.e. dbl, twin or family)
B&B: £27.50 to £35. **Evening meal:** £15
Packed lunch: £4. **Smoking:** Only in bar lounge.

Pubs and restaurants: Less than 1km.
Distance from C&C: 1km.
ETC, **4 diamonds**.
   Family run with spectacular coastal and country views, secure indoor cycle storage, drying facilities, home-cooked meals and a comfortable lounge bar. Ground-floor suites also available.

ALANNAH HOUSE
Eileen Sutherland, 84 Church St, Berwick, TD15 1DU
T:+44 (0)1289 307252
E: eileenandian@alannahhouse.freeserve.co.uk
W: www.alannahhouse.co.uk
Rooms: 3 – 1 dbl, 1 twin, 1 family. **B&B:** £24 to £27
Evening meal: No. **Packed lunch:** £4.50
ETC **4-diamonds** and **silver award.**
   Just 100m from pubs and restaurants and 200m from the route. This 300 year old building used to be the married quarters for Berwick Barracks. Rooms are ensuite with colour TVs. Central location.

ORKNEY GUEST HOUSE
37 Woolmarket, Berwick, TD15 1DH
T:+44 (0)1289 331710
E: orkneyguesthouse@yahoo.co.uk
Rooms: 5 – 3 dbl, 1 twin, 1 family.
B&B: £18 to £23.
Evening meal: No
Packed lunch: £3 to £5.
Smoking: Yes
Distance from C&C: On route with pubs and restaurants nearby.
ETC **2-diamonds**.
   Comfortable town house in central location. Tea/coffee facilities and TV in all rooms. En-suite available. Yard for bikes and all rooms can be let as singles.

COBBLED YARD HOTEL

Fred & Lynda Miller,
40 Walkergate,
Berwick, TD15 1DJ
T:+44 (0)1289 308407.
F:+44 (0)1289 330623
E: cobbledyardhotel@berwick35fsnet.co.uk
W: www.cobbledyardhotel.com
Rooms: 8 – 2 dbl, 3 twins, 3 family.
B&B: £30 to £35
Evening meal: £3.95 to £11.95
Packed lunch: £3, £5, £10 depending upon requirements
Smoking: Yes.
Own bar
Distance from C&C: On route with pubs and restaurants nearby.
ETC **3-diamonds**

Central and easy to find, just one minute's walk from the town's main street. Warm and friendly atmosphere. Hotel surrounded by Elizabethan walls and ramparts. Well run family affair with bike lock-up.

BRIDGE VIEW,

Lynda Weatherley, 14 Tweed St,
Berwick, TD15 1NG
T:+44 (0)1289 308098
E: lynda@weatherley.freeserve.co.uk
Rooms: 2 – 1 single, 1 dbl, twin or family.
B&B: £22.50 to £35
Evening meal: No.
Packed lunch: £3 to £5
Smoking: No
Distance from C&C: On route, 20m to nearest pubs and restaurants.
ETC **4-diamonds**

Georgian house situated near the railway and town centre and just minutes from the beach. English breakfast using home-made jams and all-local produce.

RAVENSHOLME HOTEL

Carole & Robert Wood,
34-36 Ravensdowne,
Berwick,
TD15 1DQ
T:+44 (0)1289 308869
Rooms: 8 – 2 single, 2 family, 1 dbl, 3 twin.
B&B: £30
Evening meal (on request): £5.95 to £10.95
Packed lunch: £3.50
Smoking: Yes
Own bar

Attractive Georgian town house between the borough's town hall and the historic walls. It is only one minute's walk from the centre and all bedrooms are ensuite with TV and tea, coffee etc facilities.

TWEED VIEW HOUSE

Eileen Dobson,
East Ord,
Berwick,
TD15 2NS
T:+44 (0)1289 332378
E: khdobson@aol.com
W: www.tweedview.8k.com
Rooms: 3 – 1 single, 2 family.
B&B: £20 to £25
Evening meals: No – pub 200m does food.
Packed lunch: £3
Smoking: No.
Distance from C&C: 1.5km from route just off the A698.
ETC **4-diamonds**

Friendly, family home overlooking the green in the quiet village of East Ord. Super views of Halidon Hill. Locked, alarmed garage for bikes.

BERWICK BACKPACKERS

Ian Cappell & Angela Sampson,
56 Bridge St, Berwick TD15 1AQ
T/F: 01289 331481
E: bkbackpacker@aol.com
W: www.bkpacker.co.uk

Rooms: 4 - a 6-bedded dorm, 1 twin, 1 single, 1 triple
Rates: £10 - £15
Evening meal: No. **Packed lunch:** No. **Smoking:** No.

This is a small, family run hostel in the heart of town. It's part of the Elizabethan walls and is within a stone's throw of the Barrels ale house and the Magna Tandoori. One of the least expensive stop-off on the route.

There are plenty of restaurants and pubs in Berwick. Just go and take your pick.

Part II

INTO SCOTLAND

Now it's time to head inland on the second half of the journey. The path takes you out past Berwick Castle, past the station, where we left off the route description *(see p.67)*. You now cross the bridge over the rail lines and head up the incline of Castle Terrace. Here a sign post takes you down a track to the left, running parallel with the A1 at Letham Shank. After less than 2km you cross (carefully) this ghastly road and head along the B6461. If you fancy taking a diversion around Paxton House, follow Route 68 – it brings you back on Route 1 and the B6461 at **South Paxton Mains**.

Otherwise, just follow the road running parallel with the glorious Tweed, traversing the Whiteadder, until you cross the border 2.5km down the road. Watch out for a sharp left a couple more km further on, taking you past Tweedhill, Chain Bridge House and the Union Suspension Bridge. Half-way across the Tweed, you are once again back in England.

You now pass the Honey Farm and follow the minor road around the outskirts of **Horncliffe**.

A good spot to stop for a pint and/or some food is the **FISHERS ARMS** *(**T:**+44 (0)1289 386866) at Horncliffe. Take a right into the village and it's just a minute away – a small coaching inn dating from 1760, with a roaring log fire for cold days (a common occurrence in this part of the world). Andrew Miller, the proprietor-chef, serves everything from snacks to steaks, and cask conditioned ale. Lunches 12-2; dinners 7-9.*

NORHAM

From here it's about 6km to the ancient and once important community of Norham. The Norman church of St Cuthbert, down by the banks of the Tweed, faces the castle across the triangular village green. The castle itself has a spectacularly violent past, as its ruined state attests. It is a noble wreck, the obvious victim of war and neglect, but is nonetheless a fine sight. Having been left on its knees in smouldering ruins, this architectural supplicant poignantly conjures up the whiff of smoke and echoes to the cry of battle.

Originally built in 1121 by the Bishop of Durham, it was fought over constantly. In 1318 Robert Bruce laid siege to it with the latest artillery while he was busily engaged in wasting the rest of Northumberland. The siege of Norham went on for one year, without success. A seven month attempt in 1319 also foundered, while three further sieges also failed to deliver the castle to the Scots.

However, in 1513 Henry VIII invaded France, so James IV of Scotland took the opportunity – with the support of the French – of crossing the Tweed and, by August 22, was besieging Norham. Two days' cannoning succeeded where all the sieges had failed. It surrendered on August 29, and since then has looked much the same. No more did it stand as a northern fastness against the Scottish hordes. James moved on to capture Ford Castle and, on September 8 – the eve of the Battle of Flodden – he captured Etal Castle. But these were pyrrhic victories, for by the following afternoon he and virtually all of Scotland's nobility, plus tens of thousands of fellow kinsmen, met their fate at Flodden. Norham is a poignant testimony to the Anglo-Scottish power struggle.

The pinkish-coloured edifice rises high on the rocks above the Tweed and the view of it from the riverside near the bridge was the one chosen by Turner to paint.

DROMORE HOUSE

Sarah Frizzel, 12 Pedwell Way, Norham, Berwick, T15 2LD
T:+44 (0)1289 382313
Rooms: 3 (1 dbl, 1 twin, 1 family). **B&B:** £22
Evening meal: £10 **Packed lunch:** £3
Smoking: No **Drying facilities:** Yes
2 pubs in the village
Distance from C&C: On route.
ETC **3-diamond**.

Peaceful spot in the lovely, ancient village of Norham on the River Tweed. All the rooms have tea-making facilities and TV and are en-suite.

Above: The bridge at the border, outside Coldstream
Opposite: another border view on the Tweed.

INLAND ALONG THE TWEED

Head out of Norham on the B6470, taking it round to the right so that you cross the Tweed (and the border) again. At the cross-roads, head left to the hamlet of **Upsettlington**, where you bear right for 1.5km until the T-junction with the B6437, at which point you go left. You will soon be high enough above the Tweed to enjoy some sensational views across towards the Cheviot Hills, across the rolling landscape of pure, unspoilt, ancient Northumberland.

Cross the A6112. Less than 1km is another T-junction. Head right, then left, past Coldstream Mains, and up to the Hirsel Country Park. There is a T-junction. You can either go right to continue the route, or left into the historic Borders town of Coldstream, where there is accommodation, watering and victuals.

COLDSTREAM

This historic Borders town is just over 1km from the route and once rivalled Gretna as the marriage venue for runaway lovers.

It is also synonymous with the Coldstream Guards, a regiment of foot soldiers raised here by General Monck in 1659, to help restore the exiled monarch Charles II to the throne. They marched upon London and succeeded. To this day, the Coldstream regiment is an elite corps of the British army.

Situated on the Tweed, there is a very good and FREE local museum, with courtyard and fountain (plus toilets). The Hirsel Estate boasts a beautiful country park and craft centre with tearooms set in woodlands.

NEWCASTLE ARMS HOTEL
Neil Gillie,
50 High St,
Coldstream,
TD12 4AS
T:+44 (0)1890 882376
F:+44 (0)1890 882241
Rooms: 11 – 2 single, 3 dbl, 5 twin & 1 family (4 en-suite).
B&B: £17.50 to £26
Evening meals: £5 - £9
Packed lunch: From £3.50
Smoking: Yes, except in bedrooms.
Drying facilities.
Awaiting tourist board inspection.
This 18th century coaching inn on the town's high street is undergoing refurbishment. It is family run, has a warm welcome and friendly staff. There's a big beer garden and lock-up garage for bikes. Serves lunch as well as dinner.

CASTLE HOTEL
Diane & Andrew Hay,
11 High St,
Coldstream,
TD15 4AP
T:+44 (0)1890 882830
E: dianecuthbert@yahoo.com
Rooms: 7 – 3 dbl, 3 twin, 1 single.
B&B: £25
Evening meal: £4.20 to £10. 3-course set meal: £15
Packed lunch: £5.50
Smoking: Yes, except in bedrooms.
2-star Scottish Tourist Board
Small family run. Friendly and traditional, near the banks of
the Tweed. Bike storage.

Candy's Kitchen at 51 High St, provides a good spot for home-made cakes, scones and that local speciality, Border Tart. It is also a baguette bar, serving hot meals with a warm welcome. Take-away service too.

Head back up the lane you came down, and go just over 1km beyond where you turned left to enter Coldstream, before heading left at the sign. Cross the Leet Water and the busy A697 and continue on the same road as far as the A698, where you turn right, skirting to the left of Birgham Wood. Just up here is a charming and out of the way establishment:

FERNYRIG FARM
Anne Mills,
Birgham,
Coldstream,
TD12 4NB
T:+44 (0)1890 830251 **M:** 07779 463694
E: fernyrig@btinternet.com
W: www.fernyrig.btinternet.co.uk
Rooms: 3 – 1 dbl, 1 twin, 1 single.
B&B: £22 or £20 if sharing.
Evening meal: £15 for 3 courses with wine, coffee & mints.
Packed lunch: £4. **Smoking:** No.
Nearest pubs and restaurants: Coldstream 7km. Pub in nearby **Birgham** opening in 2003.
STB 3-star.
Traditional stone cottage in a quiet rural setting. Boiler room for drying and huge bath with lashings of hot water. Back up teams (even with dogs) welcome. Rose garden, bike sheds, stables. Ideal base also for fishing, bird watching, hunting and walking.

The route now takes a series of dog legs through **Eccles** and **Ednam**.

Ednam is less than 4km from **Kelso**, from where the route takes attractive back lanes to **Melrose**. If you're stopping off in Kelso then keep going down the B6461; if not, take the right turn 1.5km beyond Ednam, past the top end of the race course, and briefly onto the A6089. After 1km there is a well signposted left turn, following the wall of Floors Castle. Follow this to **Makerstoun**.

KELSO

This town is worth the detour, as the Michelin guide would say if it paid any attention to Britain. Its abbey, once the biggest, is now the least intact of all the great four Border ruins.

Founded in 1128 by David I, it was attacked and burned three times by Henry VIII's men during the 1540s, and on the last occasion in 1545, the Earl of Hertford butchered 100 men and 12 monks, leaving behind the ruin you see today. What is left looks modest in size, but plans stored in the Vatican Library show that this is only the extreme west end of a very large edifice.

Kelso was described by Sir Walter Scott as the most beautiful, if not the most romantic, 'village' in the whole of Scotland. There is a Continental-looking cobbled market square and some handsome Georgian and Victorian architecture.

The town's main claim to fame, apart from the astronomical cost of salmon fishing on the pool where the river Teviot flows into the Tweed, is Floors Castle, Britain's largest inhabited mansion. Home of the Dukes of Roxburghe, it was originally designed nearly 300 years ago by Vanbrugh and was built by William Adam in 1721. Golden gates were later added and prisoners from the Napoleonic wars helped build the theatre and imposing walls which surround the estate.

Floors Castle and gardens, Roxburghe Estates Office, Kelso TD5 7SF (**T**:+44 (0) 01573 223333 www.floorscastle.com Adults £5.75, senior £4.75).

If you fancy a bite to eat, there's also the **WAGON INN** *at 10, Coal Market, tucked away behind the main street, not far from the abbey. Owned by Jackie McSorley, it does a comprehensive range of pub grub, ranging from £5.95 for some of the main courses to £15.95 for a whopping T-bone steak. Serves all day. Or the lovely* **Ednam House Hotel***, where lunch can be had with unparalleled views of the Tweed.*

THE QUEENS HEAD HOTEL

Colin & Ruth McGrath,
Bridge St,
Kelso TD5 7JD
T:+44 (0)1573 224636
F:+44 (0)1573 224459
E: info@queensheadkelso.co.uk
W: www.queensheadkelso.co.uk
Rooms: 10 – 4 dbl, 2 twin, 1 single, 3 family.
B&B: £40, or £27 sharing.
Evening meal: Fully fledged restaurant. (As we went to press Gary Moore, the esteemed chef from Burts in Melrose, was moving across).
Packed lunch: circa £5 **Smoking:** No.
Oldest hotel in Kelso, this former coaching inn, with its cobbled courtyard, has been operating since 1725. Despite its antiquity, it is homely and comfortable, and serves some of the finest food in the Borders.

*There are numerous places to eat and drink, but there's only one cycle shop. **SIMON PORTEOUS (see ad on p.127)** at 30 Bridge St (**T:**+44 (0)1573 223692) provides spare parts, accessories, clothing and friendly advice.*

OSCAR'S Wine Bar & Restaurant (35-37 Horsemarket, Kelso, TD5 7HE T: +44 (0) 1573 224008). Just round the corner from the main 'piazza', Oscar's combines flavours of the Med with local produce. The *chef-patron* changes the menu daily, and makes good use of seafood and Borders and Angus meat. Open daily 5 - late.

To get out of Kelso, do not retrace your tracks. Do not cross the river; just take the A6089, signposted **Gordon** and **Edinburgh**. Go up the hill then follow the wall of Floors estate until you get to the B6397, where you go left. Continue to Makerstoun, where you go sharp right, dog-legging until you get to the B6404, where you go left. After 4km, take the right turn up to **Clintmains**. Of all the places on the route Clint Lodge has possibly the best views. And some very fine cooking.

CLINT LODGE, Heather & Bill Walker, Clinthill, St Boswells, TD6 0DZ
T:+44 (0)1835 822027 **F:**+44 (0)1835 822656
E: clintlodge@aol.com **W:** www.clintlodge.co.uk
Rooms: 5 – 4 twin/dbl, 1 single.
Plus 3-bedroom cottage which sleeps 6/7. Can be self catering or you can dine at the Lodge. Prices on cottage negotiable.
B&B: £35 to £42 **Evening meal:** £25 set menu of fresh locally sourced fare **(BYOB!) Packed lunch:** £5 to £7
STB 4-star. 2km from **Dryburgh Abbey Hotel**
One of the greatest settings in the Borders this is a family run country house offering high quality accommodation and fine local fare. Popular with golfers, walkers, shooters and fishers, so book well in advance. Cottage ideal for groups.

The Eildon Hills from Scott's View

This is a charming route with great views of the three Eildon Hills, known as Trimontium in Roman times. One legend has it that King Arthur and 1,500 of his knights are buried here, awaiting the call to return and rescue the nation.

You could take the right turn up the B6356, a steep ascent for 2km, if you fancy taking a look at Scott's View, one of the finest and most photographed places in the whole of Scotland. It looks down upon the serpent-like twists in the Tweed, and across at the Eildons.

The route drops down past **Dryburgh Abbey** and onto the Tweed once again. The abbey is **Sir Walter Scott's** final resting place, a secluded and beautiful corner tucked into a loop on the Tweed. It too was destroyed by the English in the 1540s.

Push your bike across the footbridge. You now wend your way through **Newtown St Boswells** and over the old back road to Melrose, around the foot of the Eildons.

Overleaf: River Tweed footbridge at Dryburgh

MELROSE

The most picturesque of the Borders towns and home of 7-a-side rugby. The Abbey, wrecked like the others by Henry VIII, is where Robert the Bruce's heart is said to be buried. The Abbey was further damaged by a local family, the Douglases, who used its stones to build their own house at the end of the Cloisters. Sir Walter Scott superintended the subsequent repair works.

Abbotsford, Scott's home, is 3km from Melrose. If you have the time it is well worth a trip, stuffed as it is with Scottish curios. It is a monument to 19th century Scottish triumphalism – an utter delight (**T:**+44 (0)1896 752043).

KINGS ARMS HOTEL

Mike & Helen Dalgetty,
High St,
Melrose,
TD6 9PB
T:+44 (0)1896 822143
F:+44 (0)1896 823812
E: enquiries@kingsarmsmelrose.co.uk
W: www.kingsarmsmelrose.co.uk
Rooms: 7 – 1 single, 1 dbl, 3 twin, 2 family.
B&B: £39.50 or £59.50 sharing.
Evening meal: £5.95 to £14
Packed lunch: From £3.50
Smoking: Yes, except in one dining room.
Drying: Use room radiators.
STB 3-star Inn
One of Scotland's oldest coaching inns, The Kings Arms in the High Street, was the original meeting place of Melrose Rugby Club. Owned and run by Mike and Helen, it is a lively and welcoming inn with comfortable room and good food.

Overleaf: Melrose in bloom. Flowers are popular in the Borders

BIRCH HOUSE,
Julie John, High St, Melrose TD6 9PB
T:+44 (0)1896 822391
Rooms: 3 – 1 single, 1 dbl, 1 twin. **B&B:** £19 to £23
Evening meal: No. **Packed lunch:** £3
Smoking: No. **Pubs & restaurants:** doorstep
Distance from C&C: On route. **STB 3-star**
Spacious rooms in centrally situated Georgian house. Warm
welcome, secure cycle lock up, drying facilities. Already
popular with C&C cyclists.

OLD ABBEY SCHOOL
Ann O'Neill, Waverley Rd, Melrose, TD6 9SH
T:+44 (0)1896 823432
E: oneill@abbeyschool.fsnet.co.uk
Rooms: 3 – 2 dbl, 1 twin.
B&B: £25 single, £20-£22 shared.
Evening meal: No. **Packed lunch:** £3 **Smoking:** No.
Close to pubs & restaurants. STB 3-star
Comfortable family home in 150 year old converted school
house situated within easy walking distance of the town centre
and river Tweed.

THE GABLES
Margaret Aitken, Darnick, Melrose, TD6 9AL,
T:+44 (0)1896 822479.
E: me_aitken@yahoo.co.uk
Rooms: 3 – 1 single, 1 dbl, 1 twin.
B&B: £23 single, £19 dbl. **Evening meal:** No.
Packed lunch: £3.
Smoking: No.
Pubs and restaurants: 1km. **Distance from C&C:** On route.
STB 3-star.
Detached Georgian house in peaceful surroundings where
you are assured of a friendly welcome. Secure bicycle storage
in stone outbuilding. Home baking. Lovely spot.

Left: Melrose Abbey
Above Tweed crossing near Caddonfoot

GALASHIELS

It is a pretty short hop from Melrose to Galashiels. Although the latter is not as scenic, it is a handsome town whose motto: "We dye to live and we live to die" makes reference to the now almost defunct textile industry. When I asked a shop-keeper for the best vantage point for a picture of the town, he replied without hesitation: "Wales." Unfair! *(see above)*.

The town exploded onto the map during the Industrial Revolution from the production of tweeds and woollen hosiery. The architecture and spaciousness of the buildings suggest considerable erstwhile wealth. It is now the Borders' leading town, whose other motto, 'Sour Plums', still stands. It commemorates a Border foray in 1337 when some English soldiers, caught while picking wild plums, were put to the sword. Any event involving the death of the English is cel-ebrated up here, so take note. The Battle of Flodden is neither forgotten nor forgiven!

THE LOCHCARRON CASHMERE AND WOOL CENTRE, with the Galashiels museum of the town is within the mill **T:**+44 (0)1896 751199). Factory shop.

BORDERS FAMILY HISTORY SOCIETY, within Old Gala House & Scott Gallery, where you can check census returns, births, marriages and deaths to see if you hail from the Borders (**T:**+44 (0)1896 850264).

OLD GALA HOUSE & SCOTT GALLERY, Scott Crescent, Gala TD1, dates from 1583 and is the former home of the Lairds of Galashiels. Displays and exhibitions, family history, tearooms and garden. Admission is free.

King's Hotel, Galashiels

KING'S HOTEL, Alastair & Vicky MacDonald, 56 Market St, Galashiels, TD1 3AN

T/F:+44 (0)1896 755497

E: kingshotel@talk21.com **W:** www.kingshotel.co.uk

Rooms: 11 – 5 twin, 3 dbl, 2 family, 1 single.

B&B: £28- £36 **Evening meal:** £12 to £18

Packed lunch: £3.95 to £5.95

Smoking: Lounge bar

Distance from C&C: Route passes door.

AA 2-star

First class accommodation and excellent food are the hallmark of this family-owned hotel. An ideal centre for exploring the Coast & Castles trail, not to mention other Border routes.

KIRKLANDS

Guest House
Marjorie McLauchlan,
Gala Terrace,
Galashiels,
TD1 3JT

T/F:+44 (0)1896 753762
E: kirklandsguesthouse@btinternet.com
W: www.kirklandsguesthouse.co.uk
Rooms: 3 – 1 dbl, twin; 1 single; 1 family/twin/triple.
B&B: £17.50
Evening meal: No.
Packed lunch: No.
Smoking: In designated area.
Surrounded by pubs and restaurants.
STB 2-star. The Coast & Castles cycle route passes the
front gate on the corner of Gala Terrace and Scott Crescent.
Secure, lockable storage. Provides quality accommodation and
very good value.

TARA GUEST HOUSE

Marjorie & David Allan
15 Abbotsford Rd,
Galashiels, Td1 3DR
T/F:+44 (0)1896 752987
Rooms: 6 - 1dbl, 1twin & dbl, 1 family, 1 single, 1dbl &
single, 1 twin
B&B: £15-£20
Evening meal: No
Packed lunch: from £3.50
Smoking: No.
This is a spacious, flexible arrangement in a comfortable,
homely establishment. It is ideal for groups and is only 5
minutes' walk from the centre of town. There are drying
facilities and a secure lock-up.

KERANALT

Angela & Craig Messenger
3 Bridge St., Galashiels, TD1 1SW.
T: 01896 754859.
Rooms: 3 - 2 twin, 1 treble.
B&B: £20 or £34 (sharing).
Evening meal: on request - around £5 for 2 courses.
Packed lunch: on request - £3.50.
Smoking: In TV lounge.

Happy family environment. Keranalt is in the middle of Gala, close to the pubs and restaurants. There is a locked yard for bikes, and tumble dryer for wet clothes. Under new management since end of 2002.

The way out **(see p.135)** is uphill; up Gala Terrace, then Elm Row, up steep Gala Hill along an overhung and pleasant lane that confusingly takes you south, past Hollybush and down to a crossroads, where the lane meets the B7060. Turn right, going past The Rink, some 5km or so from Gala. Head past Yair Bridge 3km west. You are quite high above the Tweed, down to your left. There are some excellent views. At Yair Bridge (take a peek at Yair, one of the Borders' finest privately owned houses) you join up with the often busy A707, which you must follow for about 3 km. Take care!

About 1km beyond **Caddonfoot** there is a little left-turn over a bridge. You're off the main road now. Head along a delightful little lane, which takes you along the Tweed, past **Ashiesteel**, **Elibank,** the castle ruins and **West Bold**. After about 11km you will be opposite **Walkerburn**, where you can stop off should you wish – a bridge conveniently crosses the Tweed by the disused railway yard. Otherwise, go straight on for 3 or 4km and you come out on the B709.

Just a few hundred metres to the left is the village of Traquair, and the famous Traquair House. Go right, and you head back across the Tweed and into **Innerleithen**. This is the last stop-off point before the long haul over the Moorfoot Hills. After that, it's Edinburgh, some 61km!

Traquair House

TRAQUAIR is a tiny hamlet (though a boom-parish 900 years ago) famous for having the oldest inhabited house in Scotland. Deeds go back to the 12th century. Traquair House was built as a castle for the kings of Scotland, and the building you see today has looked the same since the 17th century. It is full of historic treasures, secret staircases, and a priest's chamber which provided refuge for priests during a time of terror for Catholics. The mighty Bear Gates at the top of the drive were closed for the last time when Bonnie Prince Charlie fled Traquair after the Jacobite uprising was crushed at Culloden in 1746.

The Maxwell Stuart family – still in situ – swore never to open them again until a Stuart once again took the throne. You can look around the house, there's a restaurant, craft workshops, museum and brewery and a couple of rooms to let. (adult tickets: £5.60. T: +44(0)1896 830323 www.traquair.co.uk)

QUAIR VIEW *(right)*
Pat & Brian Hudson
Traquair, Innerleithen
EH44 6PL
T: +44 (0)1896 830506
M: 07719 544208
E: quairview@msn.com
Rooms: 2 – 1dbl, 1twin.
B&B: £23

Evening meal: No. **Packed lunch:** £3.50
Smoking: No. **Pubs and restaurants:** 3km.
Distance from C&C: 1km. Newly built bungalow half a mile from historic Traquair House and less than that from the World Championship downhill cycle track! Warm house, nice atmosphere.

SCHOOL HOUSE
Jennifer Caird,
Traquair,
Innerleithen,
EH44 6PL
T/F:+44 (0)1896 830425
M: 07986 682426
B&B: £20 - £22
Packed lunch: £3.50
Smoking: Limited
E:
schoolhouse@jcairdf9.co.uk
Rooms: 3 – 1 dbl, 1 twin, 1 family.
Evening meal: 6.30pm – 8pm. 3-courses for £12. **BYOB**.
Pubs and restaurants: 3km.
Distance from route: 1km.
Comfortable old school house with beautiful views on the edge of the village, garden with birds. Log fire, home cooking. Friendly dogs and cats. Lock up for bikes.

Traquair village with the rising Moorfoots

INNERLEITHEN

Just down the road is this small former spa town. The spring is known as St Ronan's Well (also the title of a Scott novel), and was briefly fabled for its healing qualities, producing a sulphurous brew similar to the baths of Harrogate. Until the spa's discovery, the place was an even tinier hamlet than Traquair.

According to the Imperial Gazetteer of Scotland (1868): "The well was a trivial, repulsive-looking fountain, bubbling up amidst a little marsh...but with remarkable suddenness, and in a way nearly unaccountable, became celebritous among valetudinarians of all classes in Edinburgh and throughout the south of Scotland. The well, in the decorations built over and around it, in the character assigned it by popular opinion, and in the influence it exerted on the village in its vicinity, now rose, as if by magic, from the status of a watery hole in a quagmire, to that of an infant competitor with the proud spas of England. In 1824, the publication of Sir Walter Scott's tale of St. Ronan's Well, greatly enhanced its celebrity, and poured down upon it some rays of that lustre which popular opinion then assigned to 'the Great Unknown.'"

And so was the proud town born. It still produces some of the finest cashmere in the world. It is also the centre of much mountain biking, with the World Championship downhill course in the nearby Elibank Forest *(see overleaf)*.

ST RONAN'S HOTEL

Catherine Ross,
High St,
Innerleithen,
EH44 6HF
T:+44 (0)1896 831487
F:+44 (0)1896 830722
E: catherine.ross@lineone.net
Rooms: 6 – 2 dbl, 2 twin, 2 family.
B&B: £20(for shared occupancy) - £35 (for single occupancy)
Evening meal: 6-10. £5.95 to £11.95
Packed lunch: £2.75
Smoking: Not in bedrooms.
Comfortable, friendly family owned hotel catering for all visitors. Safe, dry storage for bikes. Real ales and food available all day. Large beer garden.

TWEEDSIDE HOTEL

Derek & Tina Ritchie
High St.
Innerliethen
EH44 6HF
T: +44 (0) 1896 830386
Rooms: 2 - 1 dbl, 1 family (2 single & 1 dbl; ideal for group).
B&B: £21
Evening meals: £4.95 - £9.25.
Packed lunch: from £4
Smoking: Yes
This is a small family run pub/guest house on the main street through this quaint village. It is jolly and lively and boasts plenty of entertainment.

CADDON VIEW

Amar & Elena Djellil,
14 Pirn Rd,
Innerleithen,
EH44 6HH
B&B: £32 - £45
T:+44 (0)1896 830208
caddonview@aol.com
www.caddonview.co.uk

Rooms: 8 – 2 dbl, 2 twin, 2 family, 1 single.
Evening meal: £22.50-£25. **Packed lunch:** £5.50
Smoking: Only in lounge.
Pubs and restaurants nearby.
STB 4-star/ Taste of Scotland/Which Hotel Guide
Winner of best eating place in the Scottish Borders 2002.
Relaxed atmosphere and good value with very comfortable
rooms and fine dining.

PROBIKESPORT LTD.

Neil Stoddart & Tom Ferguson,
Peebles Rd, Innerleithen EH44 6QX.
T/F: +44 (0) 1896 830880
E: info@probikesport.com
W: www.probikesport.com
This is a cycle store with bunkhouse accommodation to the
rear. It is a Shamano-approved service centre offering support
services, bike hire, clothing and accessories. Accommodation is
self-catering, with room for up to 5. Kitchenette and log-
burning stove. Minimum of 2 sharing: £25. With 5 sharing:
£65. ALSO OFFERS: Local mountain bike guiding - shop is
1km from World Championship cross-country course, with
best downhill descent in the UK. You can do a guided 3,000m
descent on a £3,000 bike on the Downhill Experience Run.
Call PROGRAVITY on 07808 922478.
info@innerleithenriders.com or
www.redbullprojectdownhill.co.uk

Those who like climbing hills like the next section best. The B709 (at the bottom of the High Street on the left) often sees more cyclists than cars and takes you into a truly wild and magnificent part of the Borders and Lowlands. It follows the Leithen Water for some 8km, past the golf course and up between Black Knowe and Dod Hill, where it parts company with the river. Purists will say that this is the best part of the ride, not least because they are usually masochists, but also because it affords some of the most stunning views in southern Scotland. Look across at distant Edinburgh from just beyond Longshaw Law, or back across the rolling fastness of the Borders. It is breathtaking.

Keep following the B707 until it becomes the B7007 just beyond **Garvald Lodge**, some 16km from Innerleithen. Go through **Middleton** and wind your way past the outskirts of **Temple** village along a brief stretch of the B6372. Watch out for the signs and take a right to Carrington Mill and continue to **Carrington** village. Just out of Carrington the OS map offers a diversion to the right, going towards **Gorebridge**. The recommended route ignores this, and heads up to Aikendean and Upper Dalhousie. 2km beyond you reach the B704. Here you have two alternatives: 1) Turn left for 2km before going right down the traffic-free path. At the end, just after crossing the A7, take a sharp right then a sharp left and follow the path around **Eskbank**. Or: 2) Go straight across the B704 and continue until you get to the busy A7. Here you

Sweeping hills above Innerleithen

go left for 0.5km (on the footpath, if you prefer), until the sign takes you off to the right, then first left and on to the aforementioned path around Eskbank.

The route **(see p.136)** now takes you around the centre of **Dalkeith**, through some fairly uninspiring conurbation. Once beyond Dalkeith, the path follows a former railway line down to **Whitecraig**, where you take a left then a right down to where the path goes under the A1.

It follows the river Esk for 300m. Go over the footbridge and bear to the right, following the path down to the railway line, where it veers to the left. You are back with that old friend, the main East Coast line, whose presence provided an occasionally thundering backdrop to the Northumberland section.

As you emerge from the passage under the railway you will see the handsome 18th century spire of St Michael's Church, Inveresk. Proceed up Ferguson Drive to the Monktonhall roundabout and go straight across. Fifty metres on it does a dog leg, heading left then right through some mini-soccer pitches, following a line of lop-sided pylons that look like a procession of Horatio Nelsons. The way-marking is shoddy on this section, but if you stay alert you will see the occasional red Route 1 stickers. At the end of Macklets Avenue follow the sign for **Newcraighall** and Niddrie, and go over the rail bridge at Musselburgh rail station. You now get a good view of Arthur's Seat.

Follow the disused rail line (never far from the A1, whose smell and noise needs little introduction). To the right, beyond the pylons, is the Forth Estuary and across the water, the Kingdom of Fife, with its rolling mountains. The route now pulls round to the right, briefly running parallel with the railway line. Follow the sign to the left, at the end of Park View. At the end of Newcraighall Drive go right, into Whitehill St. Beyond the row of shops go under the disused railway bridge, and immediately left, between some bushes. Here you link up with another line of pylons, the sort which hiss and crackle, and carry 275,000 volts into the city. Go under the one which straddles the path (over the top is not recommended) and turn right into **Gilbertstoun**, before turning left at the bottom.

At Brunstane Station, cross the wooden rail bridge and follow the signs across the 'big W' car park, and through the underpass, taking the path that leads to the right. This takes you through the so-called **Magdalene Glen Community Woodlands**, a repository for litter and second rate graffiti, with great views of Asda and PCWorld to remind you that you have re-entered civilization.

Follow the bank above the burn until the main road. Cross at the Toucan and continue along the burn. At the time of going to press this section was a disgrace. Sofas, car doors, wooden warehouse pallets, supermarket trolleys, plastic buckets,

bottles, sheeting, buggies, prams and traffic cones randomly cluttered the filthy stream. The whole montage could have been entered as a giant installation for the next Turner Prize. There is a big housing estate either side, and overweight dogs with underweight owners prowl the grey-green ribbon of grass. This is not the greatest route into the Northern Europe's greatest city **(see p.136)**, but at least it doesn't last long. Soon you are skirting **Duddingston Loch** (which you can't see, owing to high stone walls) before entering a 0.5km stretch of illuminated tunnel at the foot of **Arthur's Seat** (can seats have feet?). Skirt briefly along the edge of **Holyrood Park**. Follow the path round, and across **St Leonard's St**, and into **Rankeillor St**. Cross **Clerk St** and then **Buccleuch St** then cycle along a brief stretch of **The Meadows**, before following signs up to the right into **Forest Rd**, and then **George IV Bridge**. At the end of the bridge you will see **Edinburgh Castle** to your right, at the top of the **Royal Mile**. Cross over and follow the road down to the left all the way down to The Mound. **Congratulations**! The finish line.

EDINBURGH

This is a vibrant and happening city. There is far too much to encompass here, so I'll keep it brief ! There are any number of hotels and guest houses, most of which are booked up during the Festival, so if you're coming up in August, BOOK IN ADVANCE.

I'll just give you a scattering of suggestions here, plus pubs and restaurants that I know and like in Auld Reekie. Just as I favour Newcastle's Quayside, so the water-bias crops up in Edinburgh.

The Shore area of Leith is a fine and lively spot, and there are plenty of reasonably priced places to stay around Leith Links (the original home of golf). It's one of the trendiest areas in the city, but with a decidedly rough edge.

Having said that Stockbridge, on the edge of New Town, has lots to offer. Here is but a brief selection, including a gay section, whose epicentre is roughly between these two areas.

PUBS

Malt & Hops, 45 The Shore, Leith, EH6. Friendly, cosy real ale bar. Large selection of guest ales and wide range of malt whiskies. Lunches served Mon-Fri 12-2. Seating outside.

Carrier's Quarters, 42 Bernard St, EH6. Just 100m from the Malt & Hops, this ancient pub, with its tiny bar, is friendly and welcoming, though it can get boisterous.

Kays Bar, 39 Jamaica St, EH3. On the edge of New Town, this excellent bijou establishment serves some of the best ales in Scotland. Lots to choose from. Robust and affordable lunches.

The Baillie, 2-4 St Stephen St, EH3. Round the corner from Kays, in the heart of Stockbridge. This is one of Edinburgh's finest drinking establishments, dark and subterranean, exotic and eclectic collection of locals. +44 (0) 131 225 4673.

Bow Bar, 80 West Bow, Old Town (off the Grassmarket). This is a one-room bar with old pictures and an antique feel. Good range of real ale and single malt whiskies. It's next door to the parliament's long-term temporary home.

Cumberland Bar, 1-3 Cumberland St, New Town. Warm wood panelling. In the heart of smart Edinburgh. Serves food, with vegetarian options.

Oxford Bar, 8 Young St, (New Town near Charlotte Sq). This place features in Ian Rankin's books, as it does in his life - this is his local. Popular with writers and poets. Good old fashioned boozer with Victorian parlour.

Left: a group of cyclists celebrate after completing the C&C.

ACCOMMODATION

For last minute deals and late booking offers (especially for hotels): www.edinburgh.org or book accommodation on-line at: www.visitscotland.com or call 0845 2255 121.

There are hundreds of good B&Bs in and around Edinburgh. I have chosen just a handful to get you started.

EDINBURGH EGLINTON YOUTH HOSTEL
Donna Thompson,
18 Eglinton Crescent,
EH12 5DD
T:+44 (0)131 337 1120
W: www.syha.or.uk
Beds: 150 in rooms sleeping 4 - 10. 2 family rooms.
Rates: £11.50 - £15.50 or £10.25 - £13.50 for U-18s.
Breakfast: £2.30 to £5.

HEATHERLEA
Alastair & Amalia Hutchison
13 Mayfield Gardens, EH9 2AX
T/F: +44 (0) 131 667 3958
E: al@heatherlea-guesthouse.co.uk
W: www.heatherlea-guesthouse.co.uk
Rooms: 10 – 2 single, 3 dbl, 3 twin, 2 family
B&B: from £22
Owner is a keen cyclist. Friendly service in pleasant surroundings near the foot of Arthur's Seat.

HERIOTT PARK
Gary Turner
256 Ferry Road, EH5 3AN
T: +44 (0) 131 552 3456
E: rooms@heriottpark.co.uk
W: www.heriottpark.co.uk
Rooms: 16 of all shapes and sizes, flexible combinations

B&B: from £20
Friendly, large guest house just over 2km from centre, near Botanic Garden.

HERMITAGE GUEST HOUSE
Brenda Hill
16 East Hermitage Place, Leith Links, EH6 8AB
T: +44 (0) 131 555 4868
F: +44 (0) 870 124 9537
E: info@guesthouse-edinburgh.com
W: www.guesthouse-edinburgh.com
Rooms: 6 – 1 single, 2 twin, 2 dbl, 1 family
Near Port of Leith and 3km from city centre. Lively area and great place to finish the ride.

INTERNATIONAL GUEST HOUSE
Mike Nevin
37 Mayfield Rd, EH9 2BX
T: +44 (0) 131 667 2511
F: +44 (0) 131 667 1112
E: intergh@easynet.co.uk
W: www.accommodation-edinburgh.com
Rooms: 9 – 4 single, 2 dbl, 1 twin, 2 family
B&B: from £25
Victorian guest house not far from city centre. Highly accessible.

KELLY'S GUEST HOUSE
Tony & Liz Kelly
3 Hillhouse Rd, Queensferry Rd, EH4 3QP
T: +44 (0) 131 332 3894
F: +44 (0) 131 538 0925
E: info@kellysguesthouse.cx
W: www.kellysguesthouse.cx
Rooms: 4 – 2 dbl, 1 twin, 1 family
B&B: from £25
Kelly's smart establishment is over in the West End, around 2km from the centre.

RESTAURANTS

Not so long ago it would have been hard to recommend very much. Today, there is plenty of choice.

Restaurant Martin Wishart, 54 The Shore, Leith EH6. +44 (0) 131 553 3557. If you feel like celebrating in style and have the cash (this is Edinburgh's only Michelin-starred entry), this is widely reckoned to be the best eaterie in town. Precise and intense cooking, French-style. Very reasonable lunch.

(fitz) Henry, 19 Shore Place, Leith EH6. +44 (0) 131 555 0025. Converted 19th century warehouse, this is another fine eating establishment. Favourite dishes include roasted halibut with buttered savoy cabbage and pinot noir sauce, or ravioli of salmon and smoked salmon.

Domenico's, 30 Sandport, EH6. +44 (0) 131 467 7266. Friendly, down to earth and very reasonable. Specialises in fish and pasta. This is a good, basic, family run establishment.

Shamiana, 14 Brougham St, EH3. +44 (0) 131 228 2265. My favourite Indian restaurant is near The Meadows in Toll Cross. This is the original Balti Towers, run by Nadim Butt in a truly idiosyncratic style. Get there before 9pm. Expect to be told to hurry up if you're still around much after 10pm. Simply brilliant cooking at very reasonable prices. Small, so book in advance. Do not take offence.

Numchai Thai Restaurant, 42 St Stephen St, EH3. +44 (0) 131 226 5877. Excellent and new Thai place in the heart of Stockbridge (round corner from Baillie pub above). Spicing is generous. Food is authentic and the service first class. Reasonable on the pocket.

GAY

For all round info on the club, pub, accommodation and other scenes, try www.gayedinburgh.fsnet.co.uk

Bars...

The Village
16 South Fort Street, Edinburgh EH6, **T:** 0131 478 7810
The Bar is a unique fusion of modern and traditional decor, containing a listed gantry, soft seating, and very friendly staff. Free newspapers and delicious home-cooked food. The lounge bar doubles as a small art gallery, also playing host to a wide range of diverse theme nights, from live music to tarot reading.

Cafe Habana
22 Greenside Place, Edinburgh EH1, **T:** 0131 558 1270
Located between the Playhouse Theatre and CC Bloom's makes Habana an ideal pre-club venue. A bright and cheerful establishment, with friendly staff and reasonably priced drinks.

Claremont Bar
133/135 East Claremont Street, Edinburgh EH7
T: +44 (0) 131 556 5662
A friendly local pub and restaurant, the Claremont provides a comfortable atmosphere and very reasonable prices on food and drink. The 'Men Only' night on the 1st Saturday of every month and 'Kruz', held the 3rd Saturday of every month, are both extremely popular.

Holyrood Tavern
9a Holyrood Road, Edinburgh EH8, **T:** +44 (0) 131 556 5044. Edinburgh's best kept secret. Real ale in a gay friendly atmosphere.

GAY ACCOMMODATION

ABERNETHY HOUSE
122 Mayfield Road, Edinburgh EH9.
T: +44 (0) 131 667 2526
Quietly located in a pleasant residential part of the city and within walking distance of Edinburgh's historic centre.

ARDMOR HOUSE
74 Pilrig Street, Edinburgh EH6.
T: +44 (0) 131 554 4944
Beautifully refurbished Victorian house with contemporary ambience. Within easy walking distance of gay area and centrally located for shopping and tourist attractions. All rooms en-suite with TV and hospitality tray. Non-smoking house. Rates: from £25 per person including Scottish/continental/vegetarian breakfast options

GARLANDS GUEST HOUSE
48 Pilrig Street, Edinburgh EH6.
T: +44 (0) 131 554 4205
Centrally located, well appointed guest house within 10 minutes walking distance to the gay centre. All rooms, six in total, have en-suite facilities with central heating. Rates: from £25 per person, incl. breakfast.

ELM ROW
42 Elm Row. Edinburgh, EH7.
T: +44 (0) 131556 1215
Luxury B&B only a few minutes' walk from the main gay venues. "Undivided attention for the discerning visitor," it claims. Continental and meat-free Scottish breakfasts. £35.

Dene is a local with an expansive welcome and the reputation for the best quiz on the Coast.

Renowned for their fish & chips.

Open: Mon-Sat 11am-11pm Sun 12pm-10.30pm

Food: Mon-Sat 12pm-2.30pm 6pm-9pm Sun 12pm-4pm

Regular Activities: Tue: Quiz Night

Facilities/Features: Bar & Lounge, Bar Food, Beer Garden, Big Screen, Car Park, Children Welcome, Credit Cards Accepted, Dart Board, Good Beer Guide, No Smoking Area, Sky TV

Guest Beers. Every day is a beer festival

Crown Posada

The Side, Newcastle upon Tyne. Tyne & Wear NE1 3JE

T: +44 (0) 191 2321269 **E:** posada@sjf.co.uk

This is one of the most famous pubs in the North East, where natives of Newcastle bring visitors to get an instant blast of city life. The atmosphere of debate, laughter and beer in full flood is intensified by the pub's unique shape - narrow, deep and high - into which simultaneously talking Geordies of every caste cheerfully cram themselves. As you hold on to your pint of one of six ales on offer there's much to hold your gaze: elaborate plasterwork, carved bar, panelled entrance to the sanctuary of the snug, stained glass windows and the enigmatic crown symbol (the story that the pub was bought by a Spanish Sea Captain for his mistress is just one legend). The only entertainment is renewing or making friendships. The only music comes from the jazz LP's on an old record player. This is a great jumping off (and back again) place for the Quayside round the corner. A real bar.

Open: Mon-Fri 11.00am-11pm Sat 12.00pm – 11.00pm & Sun 7.00-10.30pm

Facilities/Features: Good Beer Guide, Good Pub Guide

saddleskedaddle

Cycling holidays in some of the UK's most classic countryside

Northumberland Coast and Castles
Cotswolds Country Lanes • Lake District Discoverer
Scottish Lochs and Glens

www.skedaddle.co.uk
00 44 (0) 191 265 1110
info@skedaddle.co.uk

Biking and multi-activity holidays worldwide

SIMON PORTEOUS CYCLES

All Geared Up For :-

- Repairs - including wheel building
- Spare Parts
- Accessories
- Clothing
- Bikes by Specialized, Dawes, and Giant
- Friendly Advice

**30 Bridge Street, Kelso, Roxburghshire.
TD5 7JD. Tel/Fax. 01573 223692.**

The
Longstone House
———— Hotel ————

182 Main Street, North Sunderland, Seahouses, Northumberland, NE68 7UA
☆ ☆

A warm welcome awaits all our guests in the Longstone House Hotel,
situated directly on the Coast & Castles cycle route.

Our family run, old, licensed hotel has a reputation for fine food and ale.

We are cyclist friendly and have secure storage for bicycles by prior arrangement

Tel: 01665 720212
www.longstonehousehotel.co.uk
info@longstonehousehotel.co.uk

'BUILDING BETTER COMMUNITY FOUNDATIONS'

Charity No: 1090188 Company No: 3852539

LYNEMOUTH RESOURCE CENTRE
Bridge Road, Lynemouth, Morpeth,
Northumberland, NE61 5YJ
Tel: 01670 863000 Fax: 01670 863008
lynemouth.community.trust@in-line.fsnet.co.uk

Located right alongside cycle route 1,
Community Café - daily specials available,
toilet facilities, cycle parking,
local information, basic cycle spares (batteries,
puncture kits etc.), repair tools available,
12 PC suite with free internet access.

Current Stamping Points on the Coast & Castles Cycle Route

Get six to qualify for £10 Sustrans T-shirt

Tynemouth - Tynemouth Metro Station, Porters Coffee House, 6 Station Terrace, Tynemouth, NE30 4RE Tel 0191 2586100

Ashington - Druridge Bay Visitors Centre, Druridge Bay, Ashington, NE61 5BX Tel 01670 760968

Amble - Breeze Cycles, Coquet Garage, Coquet Street, Amble, NE56 0DN Tel 01665 710323

Seahouses - Marine Life Centre, 8-10 Main Street, Sea houses, NE65 7RG Tel 01665 721257

Seahouses - Barter Books, 67 Main Street, Seahouses, NE68 1TN Tel 01665 720330

Bamburgh - Longstone House Ltd, 23 Front Street, Bamburgh, NE69 7BW Tel 01668 214241

Bamburgh - Copper Kettle Tea Rooms, 21 Front Street, Bamburgh, NE69 7BW Tel 01668 214315

Belford - Well House Coffee Shop, 33 High Street, Belford, NE70 7NG Tel 01668 213779

Berwick-Upon-Tweed - Brilliant Cycles, Bridge Street, Berwick-Upon-Tweed, TD15 1YR Tel 01289 331476

Berwick-Upon-Tweed - Chain Bridge Honey Farm, Horncliffe, Berwick-Upon-Tweed, TD15 2XT Tel 01289 386362

Cold stream - R. Carmichael General Store, 64 High Street, TD12 4DH Tel 01890 882413

Kelso - Carolina's Coffee Shop, 45 Horsemarket, Kelso, TD5 7AA Tel 01573 226996

Kelso - Simon Porteous Cycles, 30 Bridge Street, Kelso, TD5 7JD Tel 01573223692

Kelso - Bean Machine (Organic Foods), Greatridgehall, Makerstoun, Nr Kelso, TD5 9RQ Tel 01573460346

Melrose - The Abbey Mill, Annay Road, Melrose, TD6 9LG Tel 01896 822138

Malrose - Spar, Melrose, TD6 9RQ 01896 823408

Galashliels - Halfords, Unit 3, Low Buckholmside, Galashiels, TD1 1DD Tel 01896 751290

Innerleithen - Traquair Arms Hotel, Traquair, Innerleithen, EH44 6PD Tel 01896 830229

Dalkeith - The Bike Shed, 1d Tait Street, Dalkeith EH22 1AT Tel: 0131 6541170

Edinburgh - Sustrans Scotland, 162 Fountainbridge, Edinburgh, EH3 9RX Tel 0131 624766

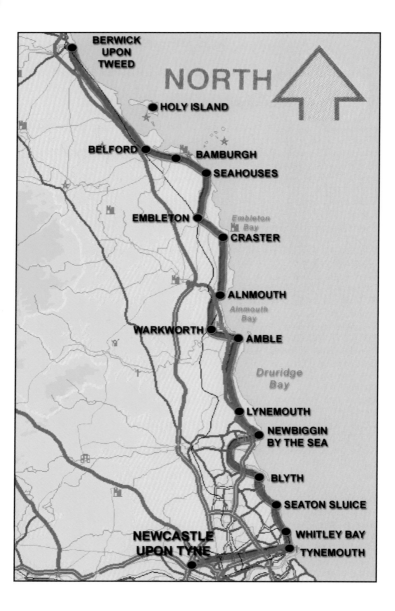

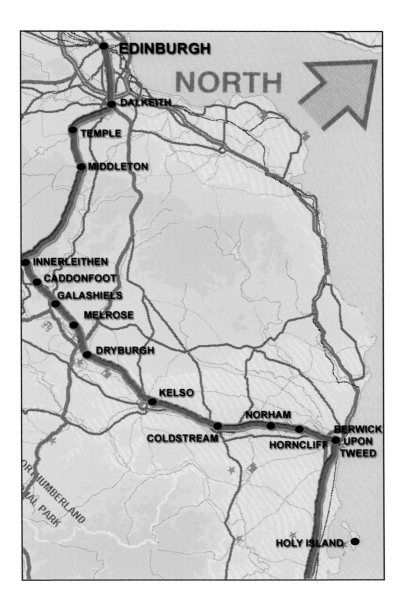

~ *Route Profile* ~

| Newcastle | Wallsend | Tynemouth | Whitley Bay | Seaton Sluice | **Blyth** |

Riding surface: ▨ - main road ▨ - minor road ▨ - traffic free

ℹ Tourist Information:
For information on accommodation and other services contact the following Tourist Information Centres:
Newcastle upon Tyne:
Newcastle Information Centre,
128 Grainger Street,
Newcastle upon Tyne, NE1 5AF
Telephone (0191) 277 8000

North Shields:
Unit 1, Royal Quays Outlet
Shopping Centre, Coble Dene,
North Shields, NE29 6DW
Telephone (0191) 200 5895

Whitley Bay:
Park Road, Whitley Bay, NE26 1EJ
Telephone (0191) 200 8535

Useful telephone numbers:
Police:
Northumbria Police
(01661) 872555
Medical:
Whitley Bay Health Centre
(0191) 253 1113
Blyth Community Hospital
(01670) 396400

Newcastle - Blyth: 33.6km (21 miles).

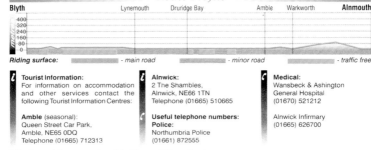

~ *Route Profile* ~

| Blyth | Lynemouth | Druridge Bay | Amble | Warkworth | **Alnmouth** |

Riding surface: ▨ - main road ▨ - minor road ▨ - traffic free

ℹ Tourist Information:
For information on accommodation and other services contact the following Tourist Information Centres:

Amble (seasonal):
Queen Street Car Park,
Amble, NE65 0DQ
Telephone (01665) 712313

Alnwick:
2 The Shambles,
Alnwick, NE66 1TN
Telephone (01665) 510665

Useful telephone numbers:
Police:
Northumbria Police
(01661) 872555

Medical:
Wansbeck & Ashington
General Hospital
(01670) 521212

Alnwick Infirmary
(01665) 626700

Blyth - Alnmouth: 44.8km (28 miles).

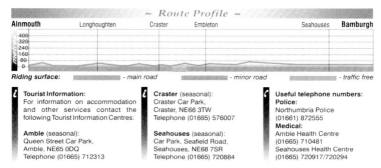

~ *Route Profile* ~

| Alnmouth | Longhoughten | Craster | Embleton | Seahouses | **Bamburgh** |

Riding surface: ▨ - main road ▨ - minor road ▨ - traffic free

ℹ Tourist Information:
For information on accommodation and other services contact the following Tourist Information Centres:

Amble (seasonal):
Queen Street Car Park,
Amble, NE65 0DQ
Telephone (01665) 712313

Craster (seasonal):
Craster Car Park,
Craster, NE66 3TW
Telephone (01665) 576007

Seahouses (seasonal):
Car Park, Seafield Road,
Seahouses, NE68 7SR
Telephone (01665) 720884

Useful telephone numbers:
Police:
Northumbria Police
(01661) 872555
Medical:
Amble Health Centre
(01665) 710481
Seahouses Health Centre
(01665) 720917/720294

Alnmouth- Bamburgh: 40km (25 miles)

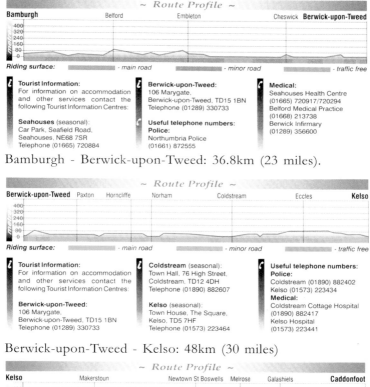

~ Route Profile ~

Bamburgh   Belford   Embleton   Cheswick **Berwick-upon-Tweed**

400
320
240
160
80
0

Riding surface: - main road   - minor road   - traffic free

Tourist Information:
For information on accommodation and other services contact the following Tourist Information Centres:

Seahouses (seasonal):
Car Park, Seafield Road,
Seahouses, NE68 7SR
Telephone (01665) 720884

Berwick-upon-Tweed:
106 Marygate,
Berwick-upon-Tweed, TD15 1BN
Telephone (01289) 330733

Useful telephone numbers:
Police:
Northumbria Police
(01661) 872555

Medical:
Seahouses Health Centre
(01665) 720917/720294
Belford Medical Practice
(01668) 213738
Berwick Infirmary
(01289) 356600

Bamburgh - Berwick-upon-Tweed: 36.8km (23 miles).

~ Route Profile ~

Berwick-upon-Tweed Paxton   Horncliffe   Norham   Coldstream   Eccles   **Kelso**

400
320
240
160
80
0

Riding surface: - main road   - minor road   - traffic free

Tourist Information:
For information on accommodation and other services contact the following Tourist Information Centres:

Berwick-upon-Tweed:
106 Marygate,
Berwick-upon-Tweed, TD15 1BN
Telephone (01289) 330733

Coldstream (seasonal):
Town Hall, 76 High Street,
Coldstream, TD12 4DH
Telephone (01890) 882607

Kelso (seasonal):
Town House, The Square,
Kelso, TD5 7HF
Telephone (01573) 223464

Useful telephone numbers:
Police:
Coldstream (01890) 882402
Kelso (01573) 223434
Medical:
Coldstream Cottage Hospital
(01890) 882417
Kelso Hospital
(01573) 223441

Berwick-upon-Tweed - Kelso: 48km (30 miles)

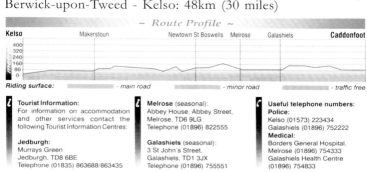

~ Route Profile ~

Kelso   Makerstoun   Newtown St Boswells   Melrose   Galashiels   **Caddonfoot**

400
320
240
160
80
0

Riding surface: - main road   - minor road   - traffic free

Tourist Information:
For information on accommodation and other services contact the following Tourist Information Centres:

Jedburgh:
Murrays Green
Jedburgh, TD8 6BE
Telephone (01835) 863688/863435

Melrose (seasonal):
Abbey House, Abbey Street,
Melrose, TD6 9LG
Telephone (01896) 822555

Galashiels (seasonal):
3 St John's Street,
Galashiels, TD1 3JX
Telephone (01896) 755551

Useful telephone numbers:
Police:
Kelso (01573) 223434
Galashiels (01896) 752222
Medical:
Borders General Hospital,
Melrose (01896) 754333
Galashiels Health Centre
(01896) 754833

Kelso - Caddonfoot: 41.6km (26 miles)

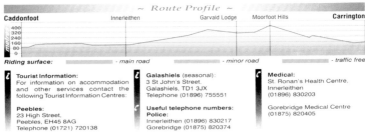

~ Route Profile ~

Caddonfoot   Innerleithen   Garvald Lodge   Moorfoot Hills   **Carrington**

Riding surface: - main road   - minor road   - traffic free

Tourist Information:
For information on accommodation and other services contact the following Tourist Information Centres:

Peebles:
23 High Street,
Peebles, EH45 8AG
Telephone (01721) 720138

Galashiels (seasonal):
3 St John's Street,
Galashiels, TD1 3JX
Telephone (01896) 755551

Useful telephone numbers:
Police:
Innerleithen (01896) 830217
Gorebridge (01875) 820374

Medical:
St. Ronan's Health Centre,
Innerleithen
(01896) 830203

Gorebridge Medical Centre
(01875) 820405

Caddonfoot - Carrington: 46.4km (29 miles).

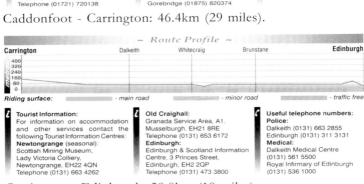

~ Route Profile ~

Carrington   Dalkeith   Whitecraig   Brunstane   **Edinburgh**

Riding surface: - main road   - minor road   - traffic free

Tourist Information:
For information on accommodation and other services contact the following Tourist Information Centres:
Newtongrange (seasonal):
Scottish Mining Museum,
Lady Victoria Colliery,
Newtongrange, EH22 4QN
Telephone (0131) 663 4262

Old Craighall:
Granada Service Area, A1,
Musselburgh, EH21 8RE
Telephone (0131) 653 6172
Edinburgh:
Edinburgh & Scotland Information Centre, 3 Princes Street,
Edinburgh, EH2 2QP
Telephone (0131) 473 3800

Useful telephone numbers:
Police:
Dalkeith (0131) 663 2855
Edinburgh (0131) 311 3131
Medical:
Dalkeith Medical Centre
(0131) 561 5500
Royal Infirmary of Edinburgh
(0131) 536 1000

Carrington - Edinburgh: 28.8km (18 miles).

The start of the ride at Newcastle (see p.19)

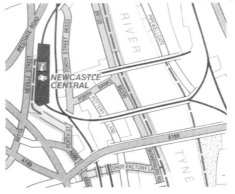

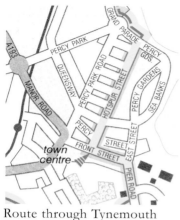

Route through Tynemouth
(see p.22)

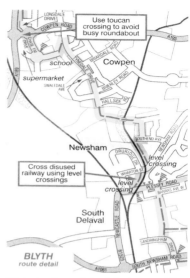

This is the tricky bit (see p.28).

Route through Berwick

(see p.69)

Leaving Gala (see p.101)

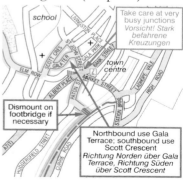

Getting through Dalkeith...(see p. 108)

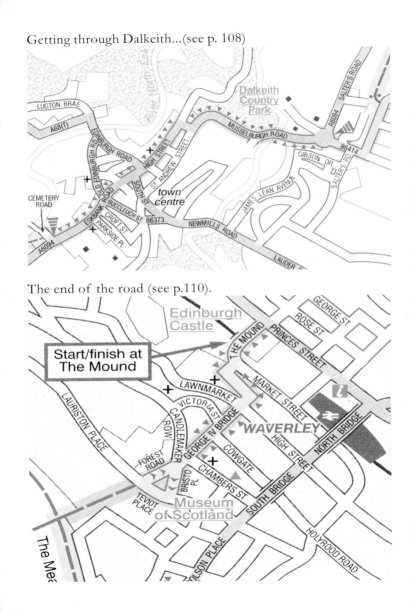

The end of the road (see p.110).

Start/finish at
The Mound